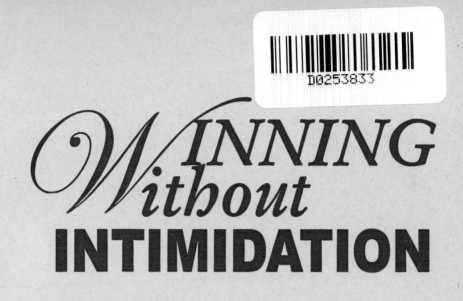

# WINNING
## Without
# INTIMIDATION

# WINNING
# Without
# INTIMIDATION

**Executive
Books**

WINNING WITHOUT INTIMIDATION
Published by
**Executive Books**
206 West Allen Street
Mechanicsburg, PA 17055
717-766-9499   800-233-2665
Fax: 717-766-6565
www.ExecutiveBooks.com

ISBN: 0-937539-55-4

Printed in the United States of America

Cover Design by Gregory A. Dixon

Gender Usage:
The author feels very strongly regarding the utilization of gender equality in his writing. The pronouns *his* and *her*, *he* and *she*, etc., have been used interchangeably.

# TABLE OF CONTENTS

*viii*

# ACKNOWLEDGMENTS

This is the most difficult section for every book because no one is more aware than I of how little I actually know, and that producing a completed book such as this is very much a team effort. So, as always, I'll do my best to mention some of the key players and realize that there will be many people not mentioned that should be. To those inadvertently left out, please forgive me and know that you are in my heart.

My family: always there for me with support and encouragement.

Our Office Manager, Ilene Vucovich: you are a true team player with exceptional organizational skills and, even more importantly, a sense of loyalty second to none. You may never leave this company to go back to work for your "second favorite employer," Mr. Klein.

My Business Manager, Ron Resnick: your incredible business skills are the main reason why I not only make money, but actually get to keep it. Thank you in advance for helping me to retire early.

All the full and part-time team members at Burg Communications, Inc.: thank you. Teamwork is what makes our team work.

John Fogg: a great friend and talented entrepreneur, you have served as a wellspring of knowledge and information regarding the publishing process.

Tina Howell: a wonderful line-editor, the extra hours you took with me on the telephone to ensure we had things "just right" is very appreciated.

Lori McCarty: the "behind-the-scenes" person. Thank you for doing all of those things that none of us realizes needs to be done.

P.J. McCarty: thank you for "coming through in the clutch."

Estelle Karlin: thank you. Your last-minute editing truly made a significant difference.

Special friends, mentors, and heroes such as Bubba and Sandy Pratt, Tim and Connie Foley, Steve and Annette Woods, and the other Interactive Distributors (you know who you are): you have all had a profound effect on my life. I'm so appreciative of our association, the wisdom you share, and the love and encouragement you give.

Robert Smith: thank you for your unselfish help and advice over the past few years.

My clients: without you I wouldn't have an audience and the pleasure of involvement in such a wonderful, rewarding, and _fun_ career such as this.

The Positive Persuasion legends such as Dale Carnegie, Les Giblin, Abraham Lincoln, etc.: as far as I'm concerned, they are the national treasures.

And of course you, the reader: for your participation, feedback, and help in making this book a bestseller.

# DEDICATION

To Mom and Dad, as always: I love you more than life itself, and treasure the fact that G-d chose me to be your son.

To my niece/goddaughter, Samantha, and nephew, Mark: you amaze me more and more every time I see you. I'm proud of you, and I love you.

Dad: this is really your book. You are my hero, my mentor, and you've taught me these principles. In fact, you taught me these principles in the very best way possible . . . you have lived them every day!

# Preface

What if you *could* get what you want . . . *when* you want it . . . and from *whom* you want it—including the difficult people we all come across?

Would that *interest* you?

Would that *excite* you?

Practically everyone would love to have that ability, wouldn't they?

Hi, my name's Bob Burg, and in studying some of the most successful men and women in modern history—Gandhi, Eleanor Roosevelt, Benjamin Franklin, Mother Teresa, President Abraham Lincoln—we notice they share many common characteristics. Each of these "winners" had a burning desire, coupled with great creativity, and a total, unshakable belief in their mission or cause. One trait which stands above all the rest is their ability to win people over to their way of thinking.

Winning through positive persuasion—*Winning Without Intimidation.*

According to *Webster's Dictionary,* to win means to succeed or *prevail* in a contest or effort; to triumph; to be victorious. To persuade is to cause someone to do something, especially by reasoning, urging or inducement. Persuasion means to *prevail upon.* When we persuade effectively, it results in others taking action. When we persuade positively, it results in others taking positive action. Persuasion does not mean manipulation.

Dr. Paul W. Swets, in his book *The Art of Talking so that People Will Listen,* says, "Manipulation aims at control, not cooperation. It results in a win/lose situation. It does not consider the good of the other party . . . In contrast to the manipulator, the persuader seeks to enhance the self esteem of the other party. The result is that people respond better because they are treated as responsible, self directing individuals."

Throughout this book are skills, techniques and attitudes regarding positive persuasion, which, when learned, internalized and applied, will make your life a whole lot easier, less stressful and much more fun.

Am I actually telling you that winning persuasion is simply a skill—that anyone can *learn* to be a winning communicator?

Yes, I am.

I know, that sounds like a bit of a stretch—but it really isn't.

Positive persuasion skills are not something most of us are born with. Like driving a car or fishing, or any other skill, not only can you learn how to do it—you can learn how to master it, too.

Mastering the art of positive persuasion . . . *Winning Without Intimidation.*

Now *that's* exciting!

I've seen statistics stating that success in most areas of life is based 10 percent on technical skills and 90 percent on people skills. From my experience, I believe that figure totally. In *Winning Without Intimidation,* you'll learn those people skills necessary to ensure that you have all the advantages needed to put that 90 percent to work for you and for others, too, day in, day out in all areas of your life and work.

I wish I could take credit for inventing these skills. I can't. I've been very fortunate not only to read and study the great masters of winning persuasion, but to grow up with and learn by example from many of them as well. I've simply taken what I've learned and applied and put it all into a simple, easy-to-use resource. Anyone can learn these skills and apply and benefit from them for the rest of their lives.

You see, on a day to day basis, winners are those people who can get what they want from others in such a way that's of genuine and lasting benefit to everyone involved—whether it's better seats at the theater or ball game, more cooperation at work and at home, the accomplishment of your life-long dream or a variety of other advantages.

There's absolutely no reason to live or work as a person who's constantly picked on, emotionally put down, taken advantage of, or made to settle for less in any way. And there's certainly no reason to ever resort to bullying or manipulating people to get what you really want, either.

What if the benefits promised in the title of this book were really attainable? They are.

I'm sure you've heard the phrase win/win. Let's do that for greater results than anyone ever thought possible. Let's create a world where everybody Wins... Without Intimidation.

Best of success,

*Bob Burg*

# Introduction

From that very first moment early in the morning, when we hit the highways and side-streets of life known as the "real world," to the moment we get home at night, we are faced with people who seem to be highly motivated and specially trained to irritate, aggravate and infuriate us with their non-helpful, often down-right rude and rotten attitudes. Know what I mean . . . ?

Sometimes it's the person next to us on the train with his newspaper spread out over two-thirds of *our* space . . . the waitperson at the restaurant who can't *wait* for us to leave . . . the surly man at the—*ahem*—customer "service" desk . . . the pre-occupied prospect you're calling . . . your boss . . . your employees . . . the hit-and-run hopeful who helps you spill your coffee on the way to work . . . the list runs on and on.

Don't get me wrong. It isn't that everyone alive is nasty or an example of bad manners, but I just read that 61 percent of the American public thinks their fellow citizens are rude! If they're right, that means you'll probably be mistreated by over half the people you come in contact with today!

I know most people are genuinely nice. But they're not the ones who make our pursuit of happiness difficult.

So what do you do . . . ?

Actually, there are only two choices: One is to get down on their level—right there in the gutter of people skills. You can fight with them, argue with them. Show them they can't push you around.

Of course, if you do that, you still might not get what you want. Even if you do, you'll probably feel worse about yourself and in the process make an enemy for life, which can make dealing with that person in the future even harder than before.

Here's the other choice: *You can win.*

1

When I use the word "win," I don't mean winning by making the other person lose. Far from it. In fact, just the opposite. I mean getting what you want from that person while making him or her feel really good about you and the situation at hand. What a great feeling of accomplishment that is!

My dad always taught us the words of the Post-Biblical scholar, Simeon ben Zoma:

"Who is a mighty person?"

The answer?

"One who can control their emotions and make of an enemy a friend."

In this book, that's just what we're going to learn how to do. It will increase your effectiveness with loved ones, strangers, associates and anyone else with whom you come in contact in all kinds of situations.

The skills and techniques I'll show you don't work only for me. These ideas are totally transferable to anyone—and duplicatable by everyone, too.

I hear success stories all the time from people who've learned to apply these methods. Some have just recently acquired or learned them at one of my seminars, while others have already been practicing them for a long time. These techniques really work! That's one reason I suggest reading and reviewing *Winning Without Intimidation* several times, until you begin to internalize the information. That way it becomes part of your being, who you are.

You can simply read over and learn the information, but if it doesn't actually become a part of you—your heart ...your essence ...without you having to think about it—you just won't be as effective in getting what you want. It has to eventually become so internalized that it's natural for you.

You might get discouraged after a few small disappointments and then be tempted to quit altogether. Don't! Keep practicing. In a surprisingly short time, you'll inter-

2

nalize these techniques naturally, simply by reviewing the book as often as you'd like. I guarantee you'll be amazed by the results. You'll gain all the benefits promised in the title—plus many more—including such surprises as receiving more money from people and situations than you previously believed was possible.

There are several other books I'll refer to and recommend throughout *Winning Without Intimidation*. Purchase them from your local bookstore or company resource/tool catalog. Then internalize their information as well. And the very best thing you can do to master this material is to share these techniques with others. One of the most effective ways to learn and internalize information is to teach it to others.

One of my favorite books is *How To Have Confidence and Power in Dealing With People*, by Les Giblin. Giblin says that what counts is a way to get along with people, or deal with people, that will bring you personal satisfaction and at the same time not trample on the egos of those you deal with. I love his definition of "human relations." He says it's the science of dealing with people in such a way that your ego and their ego remains intact.

Isn't that great!

One thing in particular Giblin said is that influencing people is an art, not a gimmick. And he's 100 percent correct! Oh sure, every so often a gimmick—as insincere as it may be—is going to work, but in the long run, by relying on superficial gimmicks, you're lowering the odds of consistent success. Just think about this for a moment: Do you really want to internalize a gimmick and make it part of who you are?

What I'm writing about in this book are the principles of *Winning Without Intimidation*. You'll probably be surprised at the fact that much of what we look at here will be familiar, because you've heard or read part of it before, possibly many times. But let's take it a step further. I'm going to show how these principles can be applied as part of a *system* to work consistently—and effortlessly—throughout your entire life and work.

Let's begin by looking at a couple of basic principles which will help you understand people, why they act the way they do and how that can lead to increasing your own effectiveness in this area.

First, here's one of the most basic principles of human nature, which if you can keep in mind—*all the time*—will help you immeasurably in your quest toward *Winning Without Intimidation.*

If you are now, or ever have been, involved in any type of professional sales, you already know the following principle. It was one of the first principles you learned in Sales Training 101. This principle is universal: It holds true for me, for you, and for practically everyone else on this planet. Although, while we're in the act of doing this, we are the first ones to deny it.

All right, enough suspense. Here's the principle:

**We, as human beings, act out of emotion, not logic.**

If you've had any type of sales training you already know this and you've had all the real world examples thrown at you to prove it's true. You understand it and you believe it. That's important, because from now on, I want you to always keep it in mind:

**Human beings act out of emotion, not logic.**

I believe we all are in sales whether we do it professionally or not. After all, we sell ideas all the time, don't we?

Spouses sell their significants on doing what they want. Parents sell children on being respectful, going to

4

bed on time and staying away from drugs. Children sell parents on buying them that toy or letting them stay out past 11:00 pm. Teachers sell students on learning, and students sell teachers on excuses as to why they didn't hand in the assignment. Yes, clearly, we all sell for a living.

If you're not directly involved in selling a product or service, it may be hard to imagine that you buy things based on emotion, not logic. After all, you consider yourself to be a very logical person, don't you? And you probably are. I'd like to think the same about myself.

The fact is, you and I buy on *emotion*.

This is a very, very important concept to understand. It is the basis for this system. The reason I'm stressing the point is that it'll be very difficult for you to learn and master the following techniques without it.

Here's basically how it works. We make decisions based on several types of emotions, but it can all be boiled down into two main ones:

The desire for pleasure.

The avoidance of pain.

We decide what we're going to do (buy or not buy a product, service, concept, idea) based on those two factors. Then we back up our emotional decision with a logical reason. It's known as rationalization.

Ultra-successful entrepreneur and best-selling author Dexter Yager says, "If we break up the word rationalize, it becomes rational lies." That's what we sometimes tell ourselves, isn't it?

Let me give you an excellent example of an emotional buying decision backed by rational lies, or "logic:"

Years ago in my "salad days"—so-called mainly because that's about all I could afford to eat—I faced a dilemma pretty much every day at about 5:00 p.m. I was starving! The challenge was I didn't have much money, so I always ate what cost the least. Not surprisingly, I never felt quite satisfied after the meal.

One day, on my way home from work, I passed a steakhouse. *Umm Um!* The very thought of that succulent, juicy steak, that baked potato loaded with butter and sour cream. The soft, warm freshly baked bread. (This was years ago, before we became as concerned as we are today with fatty food intake, but you know what, I was so hungry, it wouldn't have mattered anyway!)

I stopped in front of that steakhouse—but not to actually go in and eat; I knew I couldn't afford that. I knew if I did, I would have hardly any money left until the next payday, and that was way far away. But I could at least look at the place from the outside—couldn't I? I could just stand there and smell it—no charge—right?

RATIONAL LIE #1.

Then I thought, why not go in and just look at a menu. You know, just see what they've got. Hey, one day, I'll actually be able to afford this kind of food and, gosh darn it, I need to be able to picture it. That will give me real incentive to work even harder. Powerful motivation—right?

RATIONAL LIE #2.

Once inside, I thought, and this was *kind* of true, if I was to eat a hearty meal such as this, it would give me the strength to work even harder the next day. All that protein in the meat would be good for me. After all, I didn't want to get too thin. And the potato: Why, the skin alone has vitamins everyone knows and needs. And, and . . .

RATIONAL LIE #3.

Those were all rational lies, weren't they? That was the logic I used to back my emotional decision, which was to tear into that steak.

(By the way, that was the *best-tasting* steak I ever ate!)

Have you ever done something like that?

You and I do it all the time. Oh, not necessarily to that extent. At least I hope not! But think about every major decision or choice you've ever made: Buying your home or car . . . Getting married . . . Leaving a secure job . . . Using your savings or mortgaging your home to start your own business where the risk was greater and the hours longer.

Was any of that based on logic—*really*—or was it pure emotion?

Watch every decision of substance you make over the next few days. You'll find everything will be based on emotion. It will have something to do with your desire for pleasure—or your avoidance of pain. You and I will back up these emotional decisions with our "make-sense" logic.

Let's talk briefly about those two major emotions, because this subject has everything to do with *Winning Without Intimidation*. This is what makes people tick.

What kind of pleasure do we as human beings pursue?

We know about physical pleasure, such as sexual pleasure and the pleasure of eating something mouth-watering like your favorite flavor of ice cream. What about emotional pleasure—enjoying family and friends and the fun of buying toys? The list is endless. But one we'll focus on here is the pleasure of power when dealing with people, which is part of the ego. The ego *THEY* have. Oh no, not us . . . them.

Have you ever had experiences with negative, difficult people? Perhaps the person at the Registry of Motor Vehicles, the teller at the bank, the prospect who's listening to your sales presentation, the uncivil servant, your boss, fellow employees, the police officer, any and everybody else—they're into power, because it brings pleasure to their ego.

What about pain? I'm not talking about just physical pain. That's the least important for the sake of this book, since we're not looking to beat anyone up in order to get what we want and win. I want you to Win *Without Intimidation*.

What kind of pain would a person want to avoid?

How about the pain associated with getting fired? The feeling of pain that accompanies change, or having the risk of taking initiative—especially when that's not usually a requirement of that person's job? What about the pain that comes with embarrassment? Looking bad—the pain of loss of face?

In all of these, the ego comes into play. Ego is so important to all of us. You don't want to look bad to others or feel badly about yourself—do you? No one does.

People respond or react to us emotionally for two reasons: Either to gain a certain type of pleasure or to avoid a certain type of pain. Most of that centers on the ego.

Speaking of those two words, "respond" and "react," in just a bit we'll look at the vast differences between those two words and how you can use that knowledge to effectively and easily Win Without Intimidation.

Oh, remember the story I told on myself earlier regarding that steak dinner? I was working on both emotions, wasn't I? The quest for pleasure—in really, almost *desperately,* wanting that meal—and the avoidance of pain—being *soooo* hungry my stomach actually ached.

No wonder I succumbed and bought that expensive dinner. Under those circumstances, anyone else would've done the *exact... same... thing...* And it's all RATIONAL LIES!

As a postscript, had I made the decision to go to that expensive restaurant, which I clearly couldn't afford, in order to bring a date there with the idea of impressing her—would that have involved my ego as well?

You bet!

Let's set another foundation regarding a basic human principle, Cause of Action.

I first learned about this through the book, *I'm Okay, You're Okay.* The author, Dr. Thomas Harris, pointed out that each of us takes on one of three personality traits or characteristics during every conversation or interaction.

This is really fascinating stuff and I'm going to describe what Dr. Harris wrote and what it means to me in my words, with my own ideas. I suggest buying his

8

book, however, for a deeper understanding of this topic, Transactional Analysis. Another excellent book on this subject is *Games People Play* by Dr. Eric Berne. He's actually known as the Father of Transactional Analysis.

Each of us is capable of displaying three distinct personality states: the *Parent,* the *Adult* and the *Child.* These are states taken on, so to speak, and displayed by each of us, depending upon what we are feeling at any specific moment. The following is simply my interpretation of these three states and how they relate to *Winning Without Intimidation.*

The CHILD in all of us is perceived as the victim. He or she feels like a baby, put down, blamed, punished, controlled. As a result, that person is angry and looking to get even. The Child wants to get even with the person who assumes the role of the Parent.

The PARENT in all of us is usually a victim of their own upbringing, biases and environment. People in the Parent role mean well; they just don't recognize their negative communication. They don't realize that they're putting somebody down. They don't realize that they're making the other person feel bad.

The ADULT in all of us—which is the ideal—is the positive negotiator, the communicator, the respectful, honest, active listener, who's trustworthy and just . . . somebody who's easy to love and respect.

There are combinations of all three of those states within any relationship or transaction between two people. Somebody criticizes, condemns or otherwise talks down to you. They are the Parent and you are the Child. In that situation you have to know it's not something to be taken personally (as difficult as *that* may be), but first you have to bring yourself up to the Adult level in order to even put yourself in the position to Win Without Intimidation.

At the same time, you have to watch yourself and make sure you don't come across like the Parent talking

9

down to that other person, putting them in the position of the Child. They may react—not *respond*—but react negatively toward you because of the fear of, and avoidance of, pain, whether that be hurt, embarrassment, loss of face, etc.

Ideally, you want every transaction with another person to be on the level of Adult to Adult.

Easy? No.

Possible? Absolutely—with awareness, practice and work.

It's very important to keep in mind the human factor: You can't expect others to act like you do just because you know what you're doing and are in the state of mind to do it. Don't feel put down if that person doesn't respond "correctly." In this book, you'll learn how to get them there.

It takes time and effort, but you can do it. Please, don't get frustrated. Okay, get frustrated—but keep at it anyway. The rich results are worth it.

The best way to overcome frustration is to make a game out of it. As you become more proficient at *Winning Without Intimidation* in order to get what you want, when you want it, and from whom you want it, you'll be absolutely amazed at the fun you'll have with it.

I'm excited for you already!

One idea we need to hit on quickly is, as mentioned earlier, the difference between "responding" and "reacting."

I first learned this from Zig Ziglar, the internationally acclaimed author and speaker. This wisdom of Zig's really hit home for me. It alone has probably kept me out of more trouble than I care to remember.

According to Zig: To respond is positive; to react is negative.

When going to the doctor after taking some medication that worked, the doctor might say, "Ah, you *responded* well to the medication."

On the other hand, if you go in breathing heavily, with your face broken out in bumps and hives, the doctor will probably say something like, "It seems as though the medication has caused a bad *reaction.*"

It's the same in any relationship, transaction with another human being or situation in life:

If you *respond* to it, you've thought it out and acted in a mature, positive fashion.

If you *react* to it, you've let it be in control and get the best of you.

Throughout this book, I'll focus on *responding* to situations and challenges with people so that you may be in control of yourself and the situation. That way, you'll be in a position to help both yourself and that other person as you strive to master *Winning Without Intimidation.*

I need to mention a key concept that will definitely be at the very heart of this book, and that's "tact."

Tact is simply the ability to say something or make a point in such a way that the other person is not offended. This is also known as diplomacy, and of course, diplomats are responsible for employing tact in such ways as to keep their countries from going to war with each other.

I describe tact as "the language of strength."

If we could listen on tape to what we say in everyday conversations, we'd be amazed at the lack of tact and sensitivity in the way we relate to others. There's a great deal of truth in the saying, "You can catch more flies with honey than you can with vinegar."

Let's make an agreement, you and I, that we'll analyze the way we talk to others for just 21 days. If you feel you don't know how to do that—no problem. This book will supply you with the correct wording, attitude and phraseology.

A quick review:

• Human beings take action out of emotion (the desire for pleasure—the avoidance of pain) and back up that emotion with logic. We rationalize, telling ourselves *rational lies*.

• Ego is each person's individual sense of self. We must honor that throughout the process of *Winning Without Intimidation*.

• People take on one of three emotional states during every conversation or interaction: the Parent , the Adult, or the Child.

• We have a choice to respond or to react. Responding is positive and will add to your success. Reacting is negative and will have the opposite effect.

• A major player in the art of *Winning Without Intimidation* is tact!

Throughout this book we'll be looking at both long-range and short-range ideas for *Winning Without Intimidation*.

If you can establish certain feelings about you in other people—I refer to this as "know you, like you and trust you" feelings—that will cause your future battles or challenges with these people to be already half-won. That's a very important aspect of this book, since there are a certain cast of characters in your life—both major and minor players—that you must be able to deal with in a positive way again and again. We'll definitely work on that.

Then there are those short-range, one-time shots you encounter where you need to take on a challenging situation with a person you may never see again, but from whom you need something, and you need it *now*. We'll work on that one as well, and to me, that's a lot of fun.

Let's begin with long-range ideas:

### Thoughtfulness

It's a simple idea. No really incredible skills needed here, so let's just consider it a good warm-up exercise. If you employ the idea of thoughtfulness regularly and religiously, every day and in every circumstance possible, it will give you a head start toward accomplishing all the goals you're reading about in this book.

I read an interesting story in the book, *The Best of Bits & Pieces*. The story highlighted several acts of thoughtfulness. The main point being illustrated was that "thoughtfulness is a habit—a way of life well worth cultivating and practicing."

Thoughtfulness doesn't necessarily come naturally. Thoughtfulness needs to be worked on, cultivated and practiced enough so that you internalize these "thoughtful" thoughts into your essence, your very being.

That makes sense because, let's face it, it's often easier not to be thoughtful. As Master Teacher Jim Rohn says, "Easy to do.... Easy not to do." It's up to you in the short run.

In the long run, being thoughtful is a whole lot easier, both on your conscience and in the way that habit will make it easier for you to be more effective when it comes to *Winning Without Intimidation*.

One part of the story said thoughtful people don't wait for opportunities to be thoughtful—they imaginatively create numerous opportunities to make life brighter, smoother and more enjoyable for those around them.

How do you do that?

One thing that works for me is take time to hold a door open for someone, male or female, it doesn't matter . . . they'll appreciate you for it. It doesn't take long but makes a big difference, for that person and for us, as we make it into a habit.

When a baby near you in a restaurant is making just a bit more noise than is comfortable, and you see the parent looking a little embarrassed, smile and comment on how cute the baby is. I know some of you reading this might be thinking, "Baloney, the parent should get that kid out of there." Maybe they should—but are you looking to be right, or make the sale?

In this case, the sale being to Win Without Intimidation.

Another part of the story said, "The thoughtful person is quick to pay a well-deserved compliment, or to send a prompt note of congratulations to someone who has received a promotion, an honor, or some special recognition."

Thoughtful people park a bit farther from the entrance of the store or the post office, leaving the nearer space for someone who doesn't get around as easily as they do.

To that last idea, you might ask, "Why should I do that? Nobody will know why I'm parking a bit farther away, so I won't be winning anything, even *without* intimidation."

Let me offer two reasons: Number one, it's the right thing to do, which will make you feel better about yourself and will show up in your attitude towards others; number two, thoughtfulness is a habit. It *can* be cultivated and mastered.

Another thoughtful act is to give proper credit for an idea. *Sooo,* the contributing author of that particular story in *The Best of Bits & Pieces* was William A. Ward.

William, the contribution you made was to help me realize that thoughtfulness is just a habit—one that can serve everyone in *Winning Without Intimidation.* I thank you!

**Feeling the other person's feelings**
Let's do another warm-up exercise. This will help you

in your new-found ability to *respond* to situations and people—instead of to just *react*.

Remember the Native American adage about walking a mile in another person's moccasins? What does that really mean, and how can you use that wonderful piece of advice in order to Win Without Intimidation?

What if a person says or does something that offends you or doesn't fit into your model of how you like things to be done? Instead of reacting, what if you respond by immediately asking yourself, "What could possibly be happening in that person's life that has given her a major case of halitosis of the personality?"

Or, as Zig Ziglar would say, a "hardening of the attitudes."

Imagine a day in the life of this unhappy person, and maybe you can get a better idea of what she needs from you right now to make her feel good about herself and want to help you—be nice to you. (Only then can you Win Without Intimidation.)

Maybe that person came from a negative environment. As a child, there was no communication at home, or she was even mistreated. At school, she was rejected by her peers. (Mind you, this is not an excuse for her not to accept responsibility for her actions—simply a fact.) An underachiever with a terrible self-image, she hasn't had it any better in her adult life. She hates her job. Doesn't feel much better about her husband. And her kid just got thrown into a juvenile detention center for shoplifting.

How do you feel about her now?

Can you understand her lousy attitude just a little better?

The situation with this person might not be that bad . . . or it might be worse. If you can simply consider another possibility, you can *respond* to that person and her actions with compassion and understanding instead of *reacting* with hate and anger.

Let me tell you a most powerful story about making

the shift from reacting to responding. . . .

In his perennial best-seller, *The Seven Habits of Highly Effective People,* Stephen R. Covey shares an experience he had one Sunday morning on a New York subway.

Sundays are about the only time subways are peaceful in New York and this morning was no exception: People were sitting quietly, some reading their papers, some lost in thought, others catnapping as the train pulled into the station.

Suddenly, the scene was shattered as two boisterous children burst into the car. They were loud, yelling back and forth. Obnoxious, racing around, they even grabbed people's newspapers! These two were totally out of control and the man that came in with them, presumably their father, just sat there, staring at the floor of the subway car—oblivious! Talk about thought-*less* . . .

Everybody in that car was irritated by the children's behavior—*and* the father's lack of responsibility. Can you get a sense of what it must have felt like being one of the people on that subway? What would your reaction have been?

Well, Mr. Covey—whose patience had finally ended—turned to the man and said, with what I imagine was considerable restraint, "Sir, your children are really disturbing a lot of people. I wonder if you could control them a little more?"

The man looked up and around for the first time and softly told Covey, "Oh, you're right. I guess I should do something about it." Then, he explained that they had just come from the hospital where, only an hour ago, the children's mother had died. He said he didn't know what to think—and he guessed they didn't either . . .

Wham! Stephen Covey's *reaction* changed to a totally different *response* in an instant.

"Your wife just died. Oh, I'm so sorry!" he said, now with sincere sympathy and compassion. "Can you tell me about it? What can I do to help?"

If, with practice, we continually make an effort to put ourself in the other's person's moccasins, we'll have taken a giant step toward understanding, and thus *winning without intimidation.*

### People do things for their reasons, not ours

In his awesome book, *How to Win Friends and Influence People* (really a *must* read), Dale Carnegie talks about the fact that people do things for their reasons—not ours. If they're going to do something, it's because there's a benefit to their doing it. Oh, I know, people wake up early every morning to go to work even though they don't want to. But they get up every morning to go to work because they want something more than the great feeling of staying in bed—mainly, a paycheck at the end of the week.

What about people doing charity work for others? They're not deriving a benefit from it.

Sure they are! That benefit is the good feeling that comes along with doing good. Mr. Carnegie was right, people do things for their own reasons, even if that reason is simply to feel better about themselves . . . better than the feeling they would have had if they didn't do that good deed.

If there's something we need somebody to do for us which they don't *have* to do, then we had better be ready to Win Without Intimidation and give them a personal benefit, so that person feels better about doing that particular thing for us than they would feel by not doing it.

### People will do what they think you expect them to do

People will behave the way they feel you expect them to behave, and they will act the way they think you expect them to act. That can work for you either positively or negatively, depending upon your expectations.

Here's a great example many of you may have heard

before. Not only is this a true story, but I suspect it's actually been reenacted thousands of times over the years to prove and reprove the point.

A grade school teacher was going to be away for a few days. Before leaving, she met with the substitute to fill her in about the children and what she should expect of them.

The teacher told the substitute that Johnny was the smartest; Joanne, the most helpful; Jimmy and Susie, the class troublemakers—watch out for them; David never paid attention, better keep him on his toes; and so on.

And she was right on all counts.

Amazingly, when she returned and was debriefed by the substitute, everything she had told the substitute turned out to be true. Johnny *was* the smartest, Joanne, the most helpful. David did have trouble paying attention . . .

The only problem was that *the teacher had made the whole thing up.* She chose kids at random and gave them completely made-up personalities. It didn't matter. Not only had the substitute transferred her expectations into the minds and hearts of the children, but she acted towards them in such as way as to elicit their behavior in the exact way she expected.

It reminds me of the old-time Quakers: In every village, there was always an older, retired man whose job it was to greet all the strangers who came into the village. He would welcome them warmly and answer all their questions.

Visitors always asked him the same thing, "What are the people like here?" The old man always asked in return, "Why, what were they like where you came from?"

If the stranger said the people where he came from kept to themselves, were selfish and contrary and cold, the old man would reply, "They are the same here."

If the stranger said the people where he came from were friendly, open and warm-hearted, the old man would reply, "They are the same here."

In his excellent book, *How To Have Confidence and Power In Dealing With People,* which I highly recommend you read, Les Giblin cites many examples of how this works just as predictably in the grown-up world. He even quoted the great British statesman Sir Winston Churchill as saying, "I have found that the best way to get another to acquire a virtue is to *impute* it to him."

Both for long-term and immediate results, when you want to bring out a response in a person that meets your needs, you need to act towards that person as though that's how you expect them to respond. I know this sounds crazy, but as you approach a person for something you need, approach them *believing they're going to want to give it to you.*

Before you think I'm totally nuts, as though I'm saying just by thinking about it that's what will automatically happen, that isn't exactly what I'm saying. What *will* happen, however, is that when you predetermine someone's action in your own mind, you take on an attitude with that person which transfers directly into her acting that way. Before doubting this, do it with sincerity several times. I guarantee you'll walk away in amazement!

This is simply another one of those basic principles that I'll refer to throughout this book, so please keep it in mind. It happens to be one of the most powerful techniques, and we need to practice it until it becomes habit.

### The Three P's: Politeness, Patience, and Persistence

It was late morning on the day of a big exposition. I would be speaking the following day, and I—along with several other people—had rented booth space where we would market my series of audio and video tapes and books.

Ah, the books . . . There was a challenge. I'd really have to Win Without Intimidation that day—because *the books weren't there!*

I'd just found out about the situation, having had a message waiting for me at the hotel's front desk from the woman who was running our booth. This was in Toronto, Ontario, and since my books were sent via ground transportation from my publisher's Ontario division, there should not have been any challenge at all. But there was. It needed to be handled right away or the trip would be an expensive disaster!

I called the Metro Toronto Convention Center and spoke to the switchboard operator—who, as it turns out, didn't know how to connect me to the area where the booths were located! She didn't know the answer and wasn't interested in going out of her way to find it for me either.

In this kind of situation, you need to be polite, patient and persistent.

Polite because that will disarm the person, and it's a generally proper, effective and profitable way to act.

Dick Biggs, in his book *If Life Is A Balancing Act, Why Am I So Darn Clumsy*, quotes B.C. Forbes as saying, "Politeness is the hallmark of the gentleman and the gentlewoman. No single, positive characteristic will help you to advance—whether in business or society—as politeness."

Patient because we all realize that many "service" people have gotten into the habit when dealing with the public—many of whom can be very impolite, impatient and rude—of doing as little as possible and then hanging up the phone. Patience comes in handy when things don't work themselves out immediately after the first request. Then let your persistence take over.

So, be polite to that person and even thank them. "Oh, thank you. I appreciate your effort in looking for me. How would we be able to find out where they are and what their extension is?" With a smile in your voice, you might add, "I'm in really big trouble if I can't locate the right person."

This time the operator answers, with more concern than coldness, "I don't know."

Be patient. This is just how she's used to doing things.

You now say, "I really appreciate your help. I know you're doing your best. Is it possible for you to look through your listing of extensions and take a couple shots at it? I don't want to bother you, I just have to find that booth."

She's now going to make an emotional decision based on the avoidance of pain: The pain of having to keep talking to this polite, patient and persistent person, who obviously isn't going to stop until he gets what he wants.

Yes, she finally tracked down the extension and I was able to get the woman at the booth to find out from the loading dock exactly what happened. A few phone calls—and several hours later—my books arrived.

Remember the Three P's—especially with people who are not usually required to go out of their way to help. You must be Polite, Patient *and* Persistent.

### Motivating the unmotivated

Four days later, after the convention was over, I was faced with another dilemma. Due to a challenge of logistics, I would personally have to move all the books that didn't sell down to the loading dock and have them shipped from there. Getting the books down there wouldn't be that great a challenge, but the man at the dock took on the role of the working man who wasn't about to be pushed around by a guy in a suit ... I should have worn jeans.

When I first saw him, I couldn't tell whether he was one of the drivers or the guy running the operation. He was sitting on a chair reading a newspaper and drinking coffee, not looking as though he was working too hard. That should have tipped me off. Yup, he was the boss!

Here's an important tactic to keep in mind: If you don't

know, always give the person you approach a more prestigious title than he or she may actually have. Even if they correct you, they'll love you for it—and it will begin the process of *Winning Without Intimidation* on a very positive note.

If you think the person with whom you're speaking is the secretary, ask if she's the office manager. Not only will she appreciate your over-crediting her, but if that person *is* the office manager, and you ask if she is the secretary, you've got one big strike against you.

If you think the person is a host, ask if he's the manager. If you think she's the salesperson, ask if she's the sales manager. I should have asked, "Are you the Operations Director?"

Now, with that in mind, you know what I asked the man at the dock, don't you? I asked if he was one of the drivers. Wrong! I don't know why I did that. I must have had a temporary flash of insanity, because I never do that. But I did—and naturally, he wasn't happy at all.

"I'm the supervisor," he replied indignantly.

From there, however, I was able to "save the sale," the sale being to have this guy make the call to the correct shipping company, help me label the boxes correctly and then agree to be responsible for the boxes until they were picked up. The condensed version of this transaction goes like this:

I apologized and told him I should have known he was the supervisor. Then I asked him his name. He told me, and I referred to him as Mr. and his last name for the remainder of our conversation. (Most people aren't used to that and respond very positively to your showing them such respect. Also, extend your hand and say your own version of, "I'm Bob Burg." At the first opportunity, ask to be called by first name, while continuing to call him "Mr.") By doing these things with that supervisor, I put him in a position of power—something I bet he rarely encountered from a "suit."

I gave him even more of a position of power by saying, "I understand that helping me isn't your job and I wouldn't blame you if you can't do it, but I could really use your help." He grudgingly asked what I needed, and I simply took it one step at a time. Every few minutes, I would ask him questions about himself, how he got started in the business, his family, etc.

He began to warm up to me. I complimented him by telling how I really appreciated his help and that a lot of people nowadays just wouldn't take the time to put themselves out like he was. He smiled with what seemed a new-found pride in himself and his job.

He warmed up some more. In the end, he was taping my boxes, stacking them and personally speaking with the operator at the shipping company on my behalf.

He ended up doing all the work. He really helped me out, and he felt good about it, too—and I made a new friend. I also gave him a tip which he rightly earned. At first he refused to take it, but I insisted. He then thanked me for buying his lunch.

I won, and he won. That is *Winning Without Intimidation.*

What if I had tried to bully him around? Would it have worked?

What if I had threatened to talk to his boss? Maybe he'd have done the work I needed, but it would have taken longer, not have been done as well and who knows whether those boxes would have ever actually made it safely back to the publisher.

If I ever go back there again, I know he'll remember me and I'll already be one big step ahead in the game.

**"Thank you" in advance is the best insurance policy you can buy**

Thank people *before* they do something for you.

"I really appreciate you taking the time to . . ." This is

23

great insurance that they'll *make* the time to do whatever you want done. You may have even heard that a tip to a waitperson at a restaurant used to be paid *before* the meal was even served. The word tip, t - i - p, actually meant "to insure promptness."

Insurance—right? Or extortion, depending upon how you look at it. I prefer insurance.

An example of a proper time to thank someone before they start on the assignment, task or whatever, may be talking to your prospect on the telephone.

"Mr. Smith, thank you for taking a moment out of your schedule to speak with me." Or the hotel manager you need to inform about a particular challenge with the hotel: "Ms. Jackson, I appreciate your helping me with this unfortunate situation."

Maybe the mechanic who's about to work on your car: "Mr. Davis, thank you in advance for fixing this thing. Wow, do I depend on you to keep this car working right!"

One very important point: This all must be done with sincerity. Otherwise, it will come off as manipulative or overbearing. Just reflect for a moment about what you're most grateful for with this person, and go with that.

On the other hand, I once called a popular columnist at our local newspaper to ask her to lend her name to a charity event I was working on. As I said hello and told her it was nice to speak with her, she began her part of the conversation saying, "Thank you. I know you're going to be brief!" Not exactly the type of "Thank you" in advance I'm talking about.

I felt like being really brief—as in hanging up right then and there—but a charity is a charity. The cause was more important than my personal feelings, otherwise known as *ego.* I explained what I needed from her and she turned me down anyway. My point is, the way she spoke to me did not make me feel good about myself—or about her.

What if, instead, she had said, "Mr. Burg, I'm always

happy to talk to a person about supporting a worthy cause. Unfortunately I'm in a bit of a rush right now and can't talk too long. How can I be of help?"

I would have gotten right to it, made my point quickly, let her get off the phone and felt good about her and myself.

If by any chance you're thinking, "What does she care if you like her or not? She'll never need you for anything anyway!" I'll answer that one later on in the book in a section entitled "The 7 Words That Can Come Back to Haunt You."

### Acknowledging a job well done inspires a lifetime of repeated efforts

Muriel is a sweet elderly woman who works at the local supermarket in the deli section where they make sandwiches for customers at lunchtime. One day, I asked her for a roast beef sandwich—extra lean. She did a really nice job, and after eating, I walked back over to the counter and genuinely thanked her—loud enough for all the other patrons and her co-workers to hear—for the "Extra special nice job you did with my sandwich." Her eyes brightened quickly and a smile came to her face. From then on, Muriel always seemed to get a little extra meat on my sandwich—and always very lean.

The point is this: Acknowledge someone's effort after they do something for you once and they'll take great pains to do it extra, extra special for you from then on. The reason for this is very simple: First of all, most people just don't think enough to recognize a job well done, so your compliment is very appreciated. And secondly, every time Muriel goes out of her way to make a great sandwich, she's making an emotional decision to achieve pleasure— the pleasure of being respected and appreciated, which is probably not an ordinary occurrence in her life. I know that's true, because Muriel is human, and appreciation and respect aren't ordinary occurrences in the lives of people today.

On a plane back home from a speaking engagement, I asked the Delta flight attendant if she could possibly substitute some of the items in my meal for some healthier foods, since I was on another of my dieting kicks. She obliged and put together a nice, light meal for me. I gave her so much genuine appreciation for her efforts that for the remainder of the flight, she kept wanting to know what more she could do for me.

What a nice cycle of success! Make a person feel good for their efforts, and they'll want to keep proving you right. It's been said, "Behavior that gets rewarded gets repeated." Remember, the appreciation you express must be genuine, or that person will only feel manipulated instead of appreciated.

### Handling rude people on the telephone

From sales prospects to government employees, and a zillion others in between, there are times when you make a necessary important call and are met by a person who is rude and apparently lives his life for the sole purpose of making your life miserable—especially during this particular call.

Let's say you've never met him. You don't know him and he doesn't know you. He's just either not a very nice person or he's having a particularly bad day. It's the same to you either way—isn't it? After all, what do you even know about him? This is a phone call between two strangers, and possibly the only one you'll ever have.

Let's look at how to handle that person and Win Without Intimidation.

Begin by making the conscious decision to *respond* to the situation, not to *react*. Most people in this situation would react—they'd argue with the person, insult him right back, try and match him word for word and attitude for attitude or, even better, beat him at his own game.

While that may provide a temporary pleasure, in the long run, it won't work to your advantage. Not only will you probably not get what you need or want from that person, but you'll have made an enemy that might somehow come back to haunt you one day.

Make the conscious decision to respond and not react.

Next, while he is talking, complaining, yelling, being generally unhelpful or whatever, hear him out *without* interrupting. Then very sincerely say, "I'm sorry, I must have said or done something to upset you. Did I?" And then be silent.

It may take a few seconds, but usually the other person will come right back with, "No, I'm sorry, I'm just having a bad day."

You can then respond with, "Boy, I've had some of those myself, it's always a lousy feeling." Then they're yours. They know you understand. Most people simply want to be heard and understood.

The same idea goes for handling an incoming upset call, with a slight twist.

Let's say you represent a product or service and a customer calls to vehemently complain. This also works in person just as well, but let's pretend for right now that you're on the phone with them.

She calls and starts right in with everything that's wrong with you, your company, your product, your service. She even complains about your name—if she knows what it is.

Choose to respond, not react.

You know what you do? That's right . . . you listen, silently, hearing her out completely. If it's an in-person situation, nod your head understandingly every so often. When she gets through, again let her know you *understand*. "I understand you feel very strongly about this, and, quite frankly, I feel badly that this happened to you."

If appropriate, apologize. If not, don't. Just put yourself in that person's shoes. How would you feel?

When you speak this way sincerely, you'll disarm her, because she has readied herself for the *average* person who's going to shout right back and try to win through intimidation. Nine times out of ten, the person will calm down right then and you'll be able to have a conversation based on the Adult-to-Adult state of mind. If she doesn't calm down, go back to what you learned earlier about the three P's. Be Polite, Patient and Persistent. As long as you keep *yourself* in the Adult state, you'll outlast the other person's Parent or Child state and end up *Winning Without Intimidation.*

One point brought up in the previous example was letting a person have their say, hearing them out completely, without interrupting. This is another habit we all need to develop for any situation. This has always been a tough one for me, but I've made dramatic improvements in this area since making a consistent, conscious effort. You see, I can discuss anything and I naturally get so passionate about it, I just can't wait to get my point across, even if that means cutting someone off in mid-sentence. But that's worse than ineffective.

Whether you're discussing politics with a friend, taking part in a social group debate or making a sales presentation to a prospect, you've got to let whoever is talking finish their point. If not, they'll become frustrated and angry, and any point you make they will not buy—emotionally, where it counts. Interrupting and ramming home your agenda is just another form of intimidation, and it's very difficult to win that way—and you'll never get the chance to do it twice!

**Know you, like you, trust you**
In my book on business networking, *ENDLESS REFERRALS, Network Your Everyday Contacts Into Sales,* I talk about what I call the golden rule of networking, which is:

**"All things being equal, people will do business with and refer business to those people they know, like and trust."**

Nowadays, technology has leveled the playing field of price and quality. Other factors aside, it's the salesperson involved in the transaction that the consumer buys from or refers business to.

In *Winning Without Intimidation*, the Know you, Like you, Trust you rule also holds true. The difference is, if you're in a situation where you have never met the person from whom you need something, you have mere seconds to bring these feelings out and about. Right off the bat, if you can, elicit those particular feelings for yourself from the other person and you'll be more than halfway home.

If that person does not feel good about you, if they don't feel as though they know you, like you and trust you, almost anything that can stand in the way, *will* stand in the way of your getting from this person what you desire. The techniques in this book are specifically designed to establish these positive and productive feelings in the other person quickly and effectively.

### Ask for advice

Depending upon the situation, asking a person for help or advice often endears you to him and he will be only too glad to help. To understand this, let's realize that a person will make the emotional decision to help you not *for you,* but because it meets a need *for him.* And that need is the desire for pleasure.

And just what is the *pleasure* that person will be receiving?

He gets the opportunity to feel important, to feel good about himself. Why do you think wealthy, successful people often become mentors to young, eager beavers they don't even know or love and aren't related to? Primarily, the reason is that the thrill of the money or accomplishment is not the driving force for that person anymore. They're used to their own success. But to become a mentor, a hero in someone else's eyes, to share in another's success, feels really good.

The same goes for this person from whom you're asking help or advice. It makes him feel so good he'll probably want to help you, and continue to do so.

### The importance of OPS—Other People's Support

In the phenomenal book *The Magic of Thinking Big*, Dr. David Schwartz points out a basic rule for winning success: "Success depends on the support of other people. The only hurdle between you and what you want to be, is the support of others."

Let's replace the phrase "want to be" with the phrase "want to get," and then you can call it your basic rule for success through *Winning Without Intimidation*. It would now read: "The only hurdle between you and what you *want to get* is the support of others."

### Matching the other person's words

People rarely argue with themselves. When you can repeat an idea they expressed back *to* them, they will usually be in agreement. This is something really powerful which will endear you to them and make them more apt to want to give to you what you want.

Whether repeating something in that person's own words during the initial conversation, or repeating something in their *language* from an earlier conversation, this technique will work. The example that comes to my mind right away took place during the selling process.

I had been talking to a manager about doing business with his company, and he went out of his way to get me some information for the personal research I had to do before the presentation for him and his supervisor, which would be in about four months. That courtesy was something he did for all salespeople and was very nice and supportive.

I happened to meet his supervisor a couple of days later at a local business function, and I related that story to him about the manager's special efforts. The supervisor, being proud of the manager, said to me—using these exact words, ". . . and that wasn't something he *had* to do."

Several months later, about a week before my presentation, I saw the supervisor again and brought up the effort of the manager, adding the words, ". . . and that wasn't something he had to do." I immediately noticed the supervisor acting a lot friendlier and much more open with me. He didn't remember saying those exact words to me, but they were words that were comfortable to him, because they were his own phrasing. By the end of our conversation, he let me know he was looking forward to doing business with me.

It's a good idea to match words, expressions, tone, even volume, in order to speak in the other person's language.

Les Giblin says this not only proves you've been listening, but is a good way to introduce your own ideas without opposition. I definitely agree! Because people tend not to argue or even disagree with something *they* said themselves.

### An introduction to NLP—Neuro Linguistic Programming

The principle and technique of speaking to people in their own language has been brought to the fore on an even more specific basis through the technology of Neuro Linguistic Programming. Developed in the early 1970's by Richard Bandler and John Grinder, NLP is basically a way of quickly and effectively developing rapport with another person. After reading several books on the subject and taking a private NLP course, I find NLP fascinating and very helpful. In a sense, the previous example of say-

31

ing another person's words back to him was incorporating NLP. But there's a lot more to it than just that.

In NLP, we're taught that as human beings, we process information in three different manners, with usually one of these being the primary way. The three are Auditory, by hearing or sound; Visual, by sight; Kinesthetic, by touch or feeling.

Often, the words we use tell the listener either our primary method of processing information, or at least our mental state at that particular moment.

The words "I *see* what you mean" indicate that person is mainly visual or at least is presently in a visual state. The best way to respond is to also speak in a similar terminology, such as, "It *looks* good to me, too." Can you "see" how you've matched his or her state? If she says, "That comes across clear as a *bell*," that indicates the auditory, or sound state. If she is mainly kinesthetic (touch or feeling) or is at least presently in that state, she might say, "It just doesn't *feel* right to me," or "I can *feel* it in my gut."

One time I was discussing with a friend a personal challenge I was working through and said to her, "It's getting better. I can finally "feel" the light at the end of the tunnel." She, being a student of NLP, pointed out, "You are kinesthetic, aren't you? You just told me you could feel the light at the end of the tunnel. Not *see* the light, but *feel* the light." She was correct.

When you can speak in the other person's language, he is more receptive to you, often unconsciously so. There is even a way to know a person's present state by asking questions and actually watching where their eyes go. It's pretty amazing, and what I've mentioned here is just the tip of the iceberg.

One client of mine tells me that he even uses NLP techniques while teaching his Sunday School class in order to help develop a quicker rapport with his students. There are several good books and classes on the subject of NLP, and I highly recommend learning more about it. It's a great way for you to add some new technology to your *Winning Without Intimidation.*

### The "I message"
Here's another principle we all need to internalize, and you'll notice its theme resurfacing often throughout this book. It's called the "I message."

This is not to be confused with being "I oriented." In my book *ENDLESS REFERRALS, Network Your Everyday Contacts Into Sales,* I talk about the fact that when meeting someone new, we need to be "You oriented" as opposed to "I" or "me oriented."

This means focusing your attention on the other person, investing 99.9 percent of the conversation in asking that person questions about himself and his business. Ask him how to know if someone you're talking to would be a good prospect for *him.*

That's called being "You oriented," and it's always best to have that kind of attitude as you interact with people. It will certainly help in establishing a win/win relationship and eventually being able to master *Winning Without Intimidation.*

The "I message" is something totally different. This is where we put the onus of a challenge or misunderstanding upon ourselves, taking the other person off the hook, disarming her and making her more receptive to finding a solution to the challenge.

The "You message" would put the blame on her, making her defensive and less receptive to a win/win outcome, so you really want to master the "I message."

For example, you're in a discussion where the other person is not speaking to you with the appropriate consideration and respect. Instead of saying to him, "You're talking down to me and not showing me respect," (which of course is a "You message," as in *you* are wrong), you might say, "Sam, I feel upset. It might just be how I'm taking it, but it feels as though I'm being put down and not being shown the respect I feel I'm entitled to."

What you've done is put the responsibility on yourself, so Sam doesn't have to *react* defensively, while still getting your point across—loud and clear—that the appropriate behavior is not being shown and that it bothers you.

Let's look at another example. You're trying to get the bank manager to let you cash an out-of-town check without a waiting period. You feel you've been a customer long enough to be given that privilege, but the manager—who has the power to grant your request—is being stubborn and not showing appreciation for your being a loyal customer.

If you send her a "You message" by saying, "You're being totally unreasonable. Don't you appreciate the fact that I've been a loyal customer?," you're insulting her. You've also painted her into a corner where, if she gives in, she "loses." Instead, send an "I message," such as, "I really feel that, after years of loyalty to this bank, possibly I'm not appreciated as a customer of value. I've always enjoyed banking here. It might just be my interpretation, but it is very disturbing to me. Could we work this out? "

Diplomacy and tact through an "I message" will usually help you Win Without Intimidation.

In his book *How To Argue And Win Every Time*, famed attorney Gerry Spence points out the importance of phrasing a statement which ties right into the message. He suggests the "I message," "I feel upset," as opposed to the "You message," "You upset me."

"I feel sort of cheated" is an "I message." The "You message" would be, "You cheated me."

Mr. Spence relates how he lets a judge know he feels the judge is not treating him fairly. He'd never send out a "You message," such as, "You are unfair" or, "You are being rude to me." Instead, he would make his an "I message," such as, "Your Honor, I feel helpless," and then go on to explain his plight.

Yes, the "I message" takes some practice, but in the

end it will help you in your quest for *Winning Without Intimidation.*

### Defense without intimidation

The following incident took place at the local county's unemployment compensation department. I was to present the case of a young lady whom I had reason to believe was fired unfairly from her job and whose former employer was contesting her right to collect unemployment compensation. The man I'll refer to here as "the judge" was actually the head of that particular department. His decision would be final. In a sense, he would actually be the judge *and* jury.

Without going into too great detail, I decided to take her "case" for two reasons. Number one, I was familiar first-hand with the employer's reputation for dealing unethically with independent contractors and employees. Based on my personal experiences with him, the young lady's story was not particularly hard to believe.

Number two, during the first meeting between the young lady, the judge, and the employer's two representatives—one of whom I knew to be a tough cookie—our young lady (whom I'll call Jill) seemed to have gotten "railroaded."

I didn't feel comfortable with that. Jill was a friend of a friend of mine, and I felt a certain loyalty toward her. She seemed like a sparrow up against a couple of vultures, so Bob "Just Call Me Perry Mason" Burg stepped in.

When Jill came out of that first session all teary-eyed, I didn't realize my friend was going to ask me to represent her, or that it was even allowed, but I did ask her to tell me everything that happened. Jill said the employer's ruthless representative, instead of asking single questions as she was instructed to in order to determine "facts," just kept unleashing accusation after accusation, which the judge did not correct. This intimidated Jill.

Fortunately, before the session's conclusion, the judge

suddenly got called to another meeting and had to cut that hearing short and reschedule it. According to Jill, he even suggested she ought to just forget about the whole thing because she didn't have a chance of winning.

Well, we would soon see how the vultures—and the judge—would stand up to the techniques of *Winning Without Intimidation.*

As in any negotiation, I researched all the facts I could, but there wasn't much to go on. According to Jill, she and Karen, the office manager and the one I called a tough cookie, didn't get along. According to Karen, the reason Jill was fired and the reason they were trying to deny her unemployment compensation was that she had done something against the employer's wishes about a year before.

What she did—which I won't explain, as it isn't relevant but may be recognized by certain people reading this—was wrong. Definitely. It wasn't public-enemy crime number one, but it was wrong. She had been soundly admonished for it, and then it—the act—and Jill were forgiven by the owner. Over time some very negative personal feelings, unrelated to the mistake in judgment she made and for which she was forgiven, developed between her and Karen and the employer.

According to Jill, the reason she was fired was the negative personal feelings, and they were fighting her unemployment compensation for nothing more than spite.

With that in mind, I stepped into the office, met the judge, sat next to Jill and across from Karen and her witness, a former co-worker of Jill's still working for the employer. With no courtroom experience, I could depend only on the skills we are talking about in this book.

The judge asked if I had any comments or questions before we began, and I told him I did. My plan was to first establish myself to the judge as someone capable of representing a person, because I'm sure he's had many a screamer, or arguer, come in and try to play big-time

36

lawyer. I also felt the need to politely let him know that I wouldn't accept the intimidation that had apparently happened on the first go-round.

I began by respectfully laying the foundation.

"Mr. Johnson, first allow me to express my appreciation to you in allowing me to represent Ms. Alexander. I believe we can, all of us (gesturing to the opposition), provide enough information to allow you to reach a fair and just decision."

That done, it was time to make the polite, implied threat. This is intended to put some fear into the other person's heart, but showing so much respect that he does not lose face and could not be mad at me and therefore want to get even. (We could let sleeping egos lie.)

"Mr. Johnson," I said, "I'm sure this was simply a misunderstanding, but I feel it must be mentioned. I was made aware by Ms. Alexander, that after the first session she was advised to not bother pursuing this issue any more because the case was already decided. I know that's not true. You would never do that. In this day and age, all that does is get the investigative reporters from the local newspaper going and none of us needs to be bothered with that."

I could see that he got the point, and he made a point—with his mouth pointed even a little bit more towards the tape recorder he turned on—that such a thing did *not* happen and never would happen during one of *his* hearings.

I replied, "I knew it wouldn't," implying that I never had any doubts.

Here is a point worth noting: There are times when, in order to get a point across or have someone take action, you must—now here's the key word—*imply* a threat. Never threaten. Imply a threat. If you come right out and threaten, you paint the other person into a corner, along with his fragile ego. In order to save face, he must argue with you and show you who's boss. That's ego talking, and ego is a big factor in a person's emotional decision to avoid pain. You want to get your point across without making him angry or vengeful. That takes practice, but it's a skill worth perfecting.

Asking Jill the direct questions was fairly easy and straightforward; the challenge came when Karen got her opportunity to "cross-examine." Although the judge had advised each of us to ask the witnesses questions and not make statements or give opinions, Karen began to do exactly what Jill said she did last time—loudly voice a tirade of accusations.

This provided me with an opportunity to verbally object, and I did so very politely. "Mr. Johnson, I'm sure Ms. Patterson is not doing this on purpose, but it seems that rather than asking questions—as you had instructed—she's making statements."

He agreed and gently admonished her. She was *not* happy.

A nice break for our side was the fact that she had not been called on this ever before, and that was how she felt comfortable expressing herself. As she, again and again, began to make accusations, I, again and again, politely objected:

"Mr. Johnson, I believe that's not a question." He, a bit more strongly now, urged her to phrase her questions, as such—questions! This totally broke Karen's pattern and she began losing her train of thought regarding what she was going to ask.

The one touchy spot was when Karen brought up the incident where Jill was clearly wrong. When it was my turn to re-examine, I re-established the act and had Jill admit that she knew she had been wrong. In fact, I made no bones about the fact that I agreed—as would anybody—with the fact that she was wrong to have done what she did.

This is a variation of a tactic Abraham Lincoln used as an attorney. He would begin his opening statement by reviewing the opposition's case in a positive way, hitting on a few obvious points that he knew they would bring up anyway, and phrasing his statements in such a way that you might think he was actually representing the other party. This established his honesty, integrity and sense of fair play and justice with the jury.

Today, Honest Abe might be called *Winning Without Intimidation* Abe!

Do you understand what he was doing?

He was saying, "Hey, there are two sides to every story; the other team in this one, they're good people." He was simply demonstrating, "I'm presenting this out of fairness and honesty."

Very powerful. And you can apply that, too, whenever you're making your case through the techniques of *Winning Without Intimidation.*

When applying for a raise, let the boss know, "Hey, I understand where you're coming from. The budget is tough, sales are down, there isn't a lot of discretionary moneys." Right from the beginning, you've established yourself, your understanding of your boss's situation and your own base of honesty. Now you're in a position to give him or her your side of the story.

When you need to speak to the supervisor or manager of a person who somehow wronged you, resist jumping in with a barrage of accusations against the person. The supervisor gets that all the time. Be more effective by being different.

First, let her know you understand that employee probably has many challenges to deal with during the day, and they are probably just having a bad day today—that you don't blame them personally. I guarantee you that has just given you more credibility in the supervisor's mind than a hundred people complaining and being nasty. It works . . . please believe that. Remember this is another opportunity to use the Three P's: Politeness, Patience and Persistence.

So, back to our case.

I made a definite point of the fact that Jill was wrong, and then I asked if she was fired as a result.

No. . . . Why not?

Oh, your employer forgave you and simply warned you not to make the same mistake again?

And did you make the same mistake again?

No . . . And so you weren't fired for that?

No . . .

And I received a particular personal thrill by adding, "No further questions." (I felt like a real, *live* television lawyer!)

The rest is somewhat anticlimactic and repetitive regarding how the handling of this situation relates to the techniques we're discussing.

Karen was left at the end with the sole closing argument that Jill had been fired due to the incident in question and that's why she shouldn't receive unemployment compensation. Upon my closing, I politely brought up the fact that it had been established that wasn't the case, so, unless another reason could be brought forth, I felt confident that Mr. Johnson, "Would rule in the way he saw fit."

Notice what I said, not that he would "rule in our favor," but "in the way he saw fit." That gave him credit for being able to make a fair, just and intelligent decision.

After the hearing was officially over and he had made his ruling, he thanked me for *my* time. Oh yes, he ruled in Jill's favor. *Winning Without Intimidation* wins again!!!

### Let the person feel it was his idea

Would you agree that people are quicker to agree with your point of view if they feel that your point of view is also *their* point of view? If you're making a point and it's something similar to what that person said earlier, simply begin by saying, "And as you pointed out earlier . . . ," and

40

then continue on. You could also have said, "As you were saying earlier . . . , Joe, as you mentioned . . . " or a number of similar phrases.

But what if the person hadn't said that earlier?

It really doesn't matter! You can say the same thing and, so long as it isn't totally contrary to their beliefs, they'll probably remember saying it . . . even if they didn't. If you want, you can change the wording from, "as you were saying earlier" to something like, "as you might say . . . "

You didn't say they said it, you implied it. Keep in mind, you're doing this for the benefit of both of you. The best way to do that is to give the other person the credit for saying it first, even if she didn't.

I was speaking with the father of a friend of mine. Afterwards, my friend said that she noticed how, when I was explaining something to her father, I brought him into the conversation by saying, "As you mentioned earlier, the key is to . . ." And she said she could tell he was very receptive to that.

I wasn't necessarily trying to *get* something from him, and we weren't debating an issue. We were merely discussing a certain viewpoint that we happened to agree upon. Whenever I can, however, I like to make people feel as though they are as much a part of an idea as possible. That's just a good *Winning Without Intimidation* habit to get into.

### Handing over power

My friend Debbie had come to visit from California, and due to a mistake she made when checking her luggage, the luggage didn't make it to the airport where I picked her up. She was understandably upset and, since we were leaving on a trip early the next morning, was dismayed to be told that her luggage wouldn't be arriving until after midnight. Since this was not the airline's fault,

41

it would be up to her to come back down to the airport to claim her luggage.

She began to panic and, like most people, was on the verge of both pleading and arguing her case—which wasn't about to do her any good at all. I could see the airline employee already feeling the power of being able to deny her wishes.

Fortunately, I had caught on early enough and brought *Winning Without Intimidation* to the rescue.

What did I do first? I listened—*without interrupting*—to the employee recite the exact rule stating the airline absolutely did not have to deliver the luggage. It would be arriving at about 3:00 in the morning, early enough to accommodate our departure plans, but not convenient for the airline's delivery person nor for Debbie.

I agreed with the employee and said that, under the circumstances, I wouldn't blame her a bit for carrying out that rule. What was she going to do, argue with me about *agreeing* with her? No, so now she was disarmed, and her "Parent" had shifted into a more "Adult" state of mind.

At this point I asked her for help while handing over the power to her. That's important and I'll review that in a moment. It went like this, " You know, I'm in kind of a touchy spot. This isn't your problem and it's totally up to you, but I'm wondering if you might be able lead me in the right direction. We have an early morning trip tomorrow and by the time the airport opens, we should already be gone for hours in order to arrive at our destination on time."

Now come eight key words that will work almost every time—assuming that you've done a good job of winning this person over to your side to the point that they'd *like* to be able to help you. These eight words are:

**"If you can't do it, I'll definitely understand."**

Then, if appropriate, follow with the words,

**"If there's anyway you could, I'd *really* appreciate it."**

Let's review.

I gave over the power to the airline employee—power she already felt, but now it was willingly given. She was shown respect, which is what she wanted. Most people hunger for respect, and I gave it to her without question. Now that she was given the power unquestioned, she was more receptive to being interested in our problem and its solution. Then came the eight words that would challenge her, nicely, to show us she had the power to act and be our saving grace.

Those words are, "If you can't do it, I'll definitely understand." Followed by, "If there's any way you could, I'd *really* appreciate it." Say this with a genuine smile.

Said with the appropriate combination of humility and sincerity, this will work if there's anyway that person can actually pull it off—either themselves or with the help of someone else.

At approximately 3:00 the next morning, a driver in a delivery van pulled up with Debbie's luggage and even personally brought the luggage up to her guest room.

### Children are often our best teachers

Let's take a time out from actual *Winning Without Intimidation* techniques and learn a lesson on positive, long-term persuasion from a couple of kids.

When dealing with people over a period of time—whether family, friends, associates, or acquaintances—the best persuasion technique you can employ is *you*, the essence of you, from what you show that person on a continual, consistent basis. If you show people love, they'll respond to that and want to go out of their way to please you whenever possible.

The following story is from Parade Magazine's weekly

column, "TEENS: WHAT DO YOU THINK?" That week's heading was "FAVORITE LINES PARENTS SAY . . ."

Fifteen-year-old Laura Livingston of Florida wrote, "My favorite thing my parents say to me is 'I love you.' Even when I'm mad at them, I love hearing them say it. It's a common phrase in my house, but I feel lucky every time I hear it."

Sixteen-year-old Valerie Sleeter of Virginia wrote, "One piece of good advice I got from my father is, 'Everyone walks around with an invisible sign around their neck that says "Make Me Feel Important."' This was told to him one day by my late grandfather, Colonel Frank Sleeter, in our old country store. I think it is a good example of country wisdom."

I'd add that, personally, I think it's a good example of country, city, state and any other kind of wisdom. People want to be around and do things for those people who make them feel loved and important. This is another skill to keep practicing until it's internalized and part of who you are.

My guess is, before reading a book such as this, many people don't know that making people feel loved and important is a *skill*. It is—and because it is, you can learn to master it.

Do you know people, even acquaintances, who make you feel good whenever you're around them? You feel loved, or at least well-liked, don't you? They make you feel special, as though you're really important.

Don't you want to please these people? Why?

You want to for the emotional reason of desire for pleasure. What's the pleasure you desire in this case? Simply to have the opportunity to be around that person more, because we all like to feel special and loved.

How would you like to be that person? You can be.

If you internalize the skill of loving people and making them feel important and good about themselves, others will go out of their way to please you. People give what they get. If you give them love, they'll give it back to you—often magnified. Love people, and the challenge to Win Without Intimidation will be won before it has even begun!

**Allow them to decide your fate—you'll probably get the best deal**

This is another one of those techniques that works most of the time, as long as you've set up the situation correctly and won the person happily over to your side.

Let's say you're negotiating out of a position of weakness, instead of strength. Not exactly the ideal situation. If you read any good book on negotiation, the very first thing it'll tell you is the best way to negotiate is out of strength. That strength may be in the way of superior knowledge or the ability to walk away from the deal, even if you're disappointed.

Yet, as true as that is, it isn't always feasible—not in the real world.

Let's say you need something repaired on your car. You're in a hurry, or like me, you're "mechanically impaired." (I definitely have five left thumbs and know practically nothing about cars.) Or let's say immediate repair is needed on a part of your home, or you need a copying machine for your office right away.

The best way to handle these situations—since you have the need to take immediate action without the knowledge to negotiate the best price—is to employ the technique of "putting your fate in the other person's hands."

Here's how to do it:

First, we let him know how much we believe in him as a human being. Even if you just met him, you can just feel it in your gut and express that. "Joe, I know absolutely nothing about this particular situation. My ignorance in this area astounds me. I feel comfortable about you though. I don't know many things, but I happen to be an excellent judge of character. If I'm right about you—and I think I am—you're a business person, and you're also honest, ethical and fair. I'd like to just leave it up to you. I know you'll give me the lowest possible price, which will be fair to both of us, and will allow me to feel good about referring everyone I know to you."

As far back as I can remember, only one time did I ever feel as though the person I did business with in this way wasn't as fair as he could possibly be. Everyone else treated me either fairly or better.

What are some of the key ideas we used in that situation?

You showed him respect. You showed belief in him. You know he's fair, ethical and honest—and said so. People generally act according to the way they feel you *think* they're going to act.

You let him know you respect his business savvy (we all like to feel as though we're sharp business people, don't we?) and you wanted and expected him to make a profit. You also mentioned referrals, which handles the "What's in it for me factor." You also—very subtly—let him know that if he didn't treat you right, there probably would never be any more business from you nor any referrals.

Yes, with this technique you'll find yourself consistently *Winning Without Intimidation* and you'll need to do very little for it.

### Negotiating to Win Without Intimidation
Let's talk about negotiation for a moment.

One could very correctly say that this entire book is about negotiation. Let's face it, any time we want something from someone, whether it's money, an act of kindness, respect, or anything else, we are negotiating. More and more books these days are being written on win/win negotiating skills and I like that.

Pick up any one of those books or cassette programs and you'll get some practical tips for *Winning Without*

*Intimidation.* I know I find myself employing the tactics, strategies and techniques we're talking about in this book whenever I negotiate a transaction. And they work!

One division of my company is a mail order seller of items containing my favorite motivational saying written on top of a picture of a beautiful diamond. The inspirational quote has to do with persistence, staying the course, being able to get knocked on your rear end but continuing to get back up until you attain your goal and win your prize. The saying goes:

*You are beaten to Earth, well well, what's that?*
*Come up with a smiling face.*
*It's nothing against you to fall down flat,*
*But to lie there, that's disgrace.*

*The harder you're thrown, why the higher you'll bounce.*
*Be proud of your blackened eye.*
*It isn't the fact that you're licked that counts,*
*It's how did you fight, and why. . . ?*

When reciting that at my networking seminars, people would come up to me in droves afterwards, take out their pen and paper, and ask me to repeat that saying. Then, after one program, someone asked my why I had never put that saying on tee-shirts and sweatshirts and made them available for sale? I told them I didn't know why.

So, I did it. Listening to the wants of our customers is a very profitable idea.

First I produced the tee-shirts, then I developed a catalog full of items, such as mugs, greeting cards, pocket calendars, framable posters, all with this saying. It's been very successful, but the flagship product of this series is still the tee-shirt. I first began selling them right after my seminars, along with my books and tapes. The first thing I had to do to get to that point was to negotiate the best price I could from the tee-shirt company.

The people at the tee-shirt company were good people, and charged a price per unit that was probably very fair. The challenge was that it didn't give me the markup I needed to make the sale of the tee-shirts profitable enough to make the venture worthwhile for me.

Both the owner and I discussed the situation as gentlemen. I complimented him on the obviously fine quality of his shirts and his excellent reputation within the industry and community.

Have you ever heard someone in the negotiating process act as though she wanted to just beat the other person down? As if the only way to win the negotiation was to totally ruin that person financially and leave him lying on the floor—a puddle of limp, lifeless, money-losing mush? She speaks as though the quality of the person's product is less than acceptable and as though she would rather do anything in the world but buy from him . . . unless, of course, she can get the right price. She'll use phrases such as, "Take it or leave it!"

Why do people act like that? Those people do win their share of battles, but very rarely win the game . . . of life or of work.

You can't build yourself up by knocking someone else down—except in certain sports where that is literally the point of the game. But that isn't the idea of life, or work, and it certainly isn't the idea of *Winning Without Intimidation.*

By the way, you know what is fundamentally wrong with saying "Take it or leave it?"

When you say that to someone, you are directly challenging his ego. And you know that people buy emotionally—correct? Would you agree with me that many people would turn down a very good offer just to protect their egos? I've seen it happen many times.

Back to the tee-shirts:

After negotiating our best respective deals, each in our own minds, he and I were at a standstill. His final price

48

was 50 cents per unit higher than I was willing to go. He told me that the price would be difficult to lower, even though he'd really like my business.

I told him, again, very politely, that although I'd love to be able to give him my business, I just couldn't do it. I'd have to continue to shop other places, even out of state, though I'd sure rather keep my money circulating within my own local community.

He came back with one more offer: 25 cents lower. I told him I appreciated his consideration so very much, but that any way I cut it, I just couldn't go over the mark I had set down, which was still 25 cents lower than that. I said if it would help him justify his price, I'd order several hundred more tee-shirts than I was going to order originally. He stood there silently . . . not saying a word . . . thinking.

It was time to put the deal in his hands, politely letting him know I *would* walk away if I had to, but attempting to phrase it in just such a way that he would consider doing something he ordinarily would not do.

"Jim," I said, "I totally understand your situation and wouldn't feel slighted a bit if you couldn't justify coming down to this price. I have a feeling, though, that we could be doing business with each other for a long time. Why don't you take some time and think about it awhile. You know my number; give me a call when you decide. I've really enjoyed meeting with you. You're a talented, good guy." And I went back to my office not sure of what his answer would be.

My office manager didn't think it would fly. She called a friend of hers who often bought shirts for local sports teams and other community events. She didn't think we had a chance of getting that price. Thirty minutes later, we got the phone call and Jim's agreement on the deal. They turned out to be great people to deal with, even loading up a bunch of boxes of tee-shirts and delivering them right to the office for us.

To this day, I genuinely believe that a part of getting

that agreement for what was really an outstanding price was the fact that I showed the owner the proper respect and appreciation for his position and his circumstances. When you negotiate in good faith and with the proper attitude, more often than not you're going to find yourself *Winning Without Intimidation*. And remember this key point:

*For you to win, the other person has to win as well.*

I'm sure Jim made a profit, but more than that, I know he felt good about landing his new *life-long* customer.

### How to decline an offer and still Win Without Intimidation

The following story hits on an interesting point, once again dealing with showing respect—especially in a situation where many people wouldn't.

When you're involved in a negotiation and a person offers you a deal that you are simply not interested in, remain respectful no matter what. By declining an offer respectfully, you're positioned to receive "a benefit of a miscommunication."

Often companies buy a large quantity of my cassette tape program entitled *HOW TO CULTIVATE A NETWORK OF ENDLESS REFERRALS*, to be used either as resale items or tools for continuing training for their salespeople. One particular company's representative asked me if they could make a duplicate of the recording master and produce the tapes themselves. They would then give me a royalty per tape program sold. They asked this because my tapes retailed at a higher price than they were willing to pay.

Talk about something that didn't interest me at all! There was no way I'd ever do that.

But instead of laughing condescendingly or putting the representative down, which would have offended him

50

or embarrassed him or hurt his ego, I simply declined by saying, "Mr. Sanders, I appreciate your kind offer, and I feel honored you'd want to share my information with your people, but if I did that it would be unfair to all the people who distribute these and get such a substantial discount for doing so."

He looked very surprised.

Not surprised that I declined his offer, but because he didn't realize I gave distributors and quantity buyers such a major discount. He'd never thought to ask and I just figured he knew. I was wrong, he didn't know. When I told him the discounted price, he was delighted, and we agreed on the transaction right there. He became a good client.

Had I put him down—which would have been quite natural for most of us, because his offer was almost insulting—do you think we would have ever gotten to the point of understanding? Even if we had, would offending him have helped or hurt my chances of our coming to an agreement?

Declining an offer respectfully (and you could substitute the word *responsibly*) will dramatically increase your chances of *Winning Without Intimidation*.

I have, many times, after telling a prospect what I charge for a speaking engagement, been talked to as if I was committing highway robbery. I've actually been laughed at! "Ha! You're kidding! I'd *never* pay a speaker *that much!*"

I have an ego, too, so when someone does that, and then later decides they want me, they can no longer have me at the former price. Their price goes up.

But if they say, "Bob, I'd love to have you come in for us, but I just couldn't possibly pay you that kind of money," that's different. We still might not be able to work anything out together, but maybe we would. Possibly, we could arrange a slightly lesser fee with a trade-out for one of their company's products, or design a combination of a fee with guaranteed or advance product sales. I would at least—and I have often done this in these circumstances—go out of my way to find them another speaker who would do them well at a lower fee level.

It's important to decline with respect and make the other person feel good about herself. Then, if there is any chance for a positive outcome to result, the odds are far greater that's what will happen.

## Get the person from whom you want help involved in the challenge

People will be more apt to help you solve a challenge if they feel your challenge is also their challenge.

Les Giblin brought this point up beautifully in *How To Have Confidence and Power in Dealing With People*. He suggests instead of asking someone to help you with *your* challenge, make it his challenge as well, simply by asking him how *he* would solve the problem.

For instance, you're trying to figure out how to connect a gidger-gadget. You know that Tom has good mechanical skills and it would be a snap for him to make the connection. You, on the other hand, are like I am and can't put together a two-piece gadget that says, "Snap on here."

You could just come right out and ask Tom to do this for you, but unless he's a good friend or just a naturally helpful guy, he'll probably find a reason to decline. But if you say, "Tom, you're a master with your hands and I'm the worst; how would you suggest I begin to put together a gidger-gadget?" Tom—whose ego you just fed quite nicely (You just called him a master, remember?)—will probably want to show you how. And he might not stop until he's done.

Let's say you're trying to get an introduction to Deborah Durham, the decision maker of a company who could use your products. You're sure that if you could just get in to see Ms. Durham, you could have her as a very lucrative, long-term client. You know a man in the company named Steve, who personally knows Ms. Durham, but

52

you don't quite know him well enough for him necessarily to want to go out of his way for you. Instead of asking him to make the introduction, what if you just got him personally involved in the process? "Hi Steve, could I ask you for a piece of advice regarding a certain challenge I'm having?"

You've made Steve feel important—and that's good for his ego, which might cause him to be interested in how he could attain that particular pay-off of emotional pleasure.

"Sure," says Steve, "what can I do for you?"

"Well," you reply, "If you don't mind my asking, if you were an outside salesperson who needed to see Deborah Durham at your company in order to show her your products, and you just couldn't get past her secretary, what would you do? I can't figure it out."

Wow, what a challenge you've given Steve! How could a person given so much respect for his inside knowledge possibly refuse to share that information? Not that it couldn't happen, mind you, but you've certainly increased your odds of getting an introduction to Ms. Durham.

Another win!

**How to disagree and still Win Without Intimidation**

No one likes to be corrected, even when they say something that is absolutely wrong.

Your prospect tells you he would never buy your product because it doesn't have the capacity to cross-file data to the 102nd mega-degree. You know that's not true, yet, if you come right out and tell him he's wrong, he'll resent you for it.

You could convince him logically of the fact that your product not only can cross-file data to the 102nd mega-degree (whatever that means), but could also do it at the speed of light, while blindfolded—and the chances are your prospect will still say "No." He'll find a way to say "no" to protect his position anyway he has to, because he feels his ego has been bruised.

Would you agree with that? At least nine times out of 10—right? We've all watched it happen.

Your boss gives you back a report you handed in and asks you to correct one area that you know was right. You researched it, checked and double checked it and you know *it's right.*

How do you suppose your boss will respond, however, if you simply tell her she was wrong? That your report was right? Is there a chance her ego may not appreciate that and she'll find a way to make it—and you—wrong? Or look for something wrong on your next report? Unless this person is an extraordinary human being, you bet she will!

Why take a chance? Phrase your disagreement in a way she can live with and even appreciate. Take the onus off her and put it on your own "lack of understanding." This works like a charm.

When having to disagree with another person's statement in order to get your point across and get what you want, it's often best to lead into the correction with statements such as, "Correct me if I'm wrong . . ." or, "I don't understand . . ." or, "Could you clarify something for me . . . ?"

Pat tells you he can't deliver your new furniture by Friday. You could *react* by saying, "You did it the same day for Dave Sprazinski on a special delivery order!" Instead, why not *respond* with, "Joe, correct me if I'm wrong—you know these things much better than I do—weren't you able to get my friend Dave Sprazinski's furniture to him in on some sort of, I don't know, special delivery order?"

Marjorie says, "I don't like how that looks in this particular order." Two days earlier, that's exactly the order she wanted it in and correcting it would cost you a whole lot of time and money. But if you come right out and tell her that, she probably won't budge an inch.

Why not lead into your statement with, "Marjorie, could you clarify something for me, because I want you to be totally happy with my order. I interpreted what you said to look this way. It really does work great, too, your judgment was right on the mark. Can we review this step-by-step?"

Keep in mind, when you have to correct someone who is wrong, you need to do this without offending them and their ego. Use diplomatic phrases that allow you to *tactfully* move into the information you need to express in order to get agreement from that person.

### Long-term *Winning Without Intimidation* through personalized Thank You notes

Let's change speed right here and once again focus on creating some consistent, long term success with people. This tactic may seem to be a bit of an inconvenience, but it really isn't. Once you develop this success habit it will make a world of difference in your ability to Win Without Intimidation. You'll have people on your side *for life* after you do, and potential challenges may never actually surface. This habit of long-term success is simply, "writing thank you notes."

I know, we've all been taught to do that. Our moms may have insisted we write thank you notes after attending a birthday party or eating dinner over at someone's home. If you're in a selling-related field, you may have learned about thank you notes in Basic Sales Training 101. However, very few people actually write them, not realizing they are missing a golden opportunity.

When you send a note, you are remembered for a good reason—you distinguish yourself from all those who don't send notes, which is almost *everyone* else.

I've found sending thank you notes to be one of the most—if not *the* most—powerful tools in building a super huge network, both professionally and socially. I've also noticed that people with the most impressive networks are avid note writers. Does that say something? I think it does.

Not only will you be remembered by the person to whom you sent the note, you will also be remembered for having cared enough to make the effort. Show someone they matter to you, and you will matter to them.

When the air-conditioning repair person comes out to fix your unit, send her a nice, hand-written thank you note (a thank you note to her boss wouldn't be a bad idea either). If you ever need them in an emergency, there's a good chance they'll remember you and your note and come through for you.

When you've had a particularly good meal at a restaurant, drop a nice handwritten note to both the waitperson and the owner or manager. You'll most likely be treated as a VIP forever after. I can tell you, both from personal experience and the experiences of others, this works Big-Time.

If, for whatever reason, you ever need help from a police officer, be sure and send him, and his commanding officer, a thank you note. You certainly want them on your side in the event of, heaven forbid, a real emergency.

I repeat, both from personal experience and the experiences of others, this works Big-Time.

When you meet a person who may be in a position to either purchase your products or services, or refer you to others who can, send a nice, hand-written note. When salespeople do this with consistency (consistency being the key), they receive dramatic long-term, as well as often even short-term, results.

Here's how I set mine up: I went to my local quick-printer and had him design the notecard for me. It was 8 1/2 by 3 1/2 inches, on paper just a bit heavier than the usual 20 pound bond. That size will fit comfortably into a standard number 10 envelope. The card's design has my company logo on the upper right hand side and below that is my picture, because I want recipients to be able to remember who I am. The picture should be small and professional according to the image you wish to project.

A lot of people are embarrassed at first to include their

picture, but it really does help others to remember you. Remember the saying, "Out of sight, out of mind?" Below the picture is my address and phone number, and on the very bottom of the card is a short benefit statement about the product or service I provide.

Keep your information from taking up too much space. You want this note to be oriented towards the other person, not a piece that looks like an advertisement for you. That would have exactly the opposite effect from what you want. Regardless of the business you're in—or even if you're not in any particular business—set the card up the same way, but geared to your own unique situation.

If you'd like a free sample of mine, so you can take it to your local printer for easier setup, just send a self-addressed, stamped envelope to the address in the back of this book requesting Bob's notecard, and one will be sent to you promptly.

When writing the note, I suggest using a pen with blue ink. Blue ink has been proven to be more effective both business-wise and personally. The note should be kept short, simple and sweet.

For example: *Pat, Thank you so much for the super job you did with our air-conditioner. It's great to know of a service professional who really understands the meaning of "service." I'll let all our friends know about you. Thanks.* Then sign your name.

Do you think the comfort of you and your family will take precedence in the future? You can bet on it!

When I meet a potential business contact, my note will read, *Hi, Ann, Thank you. It was a pleasure meeting you at the Chamber of Commerce function. If I can ever refer business your way, I certainly will. Bob.*

When you write a nice note to the waiter and owner of the restaurant, how quickly do you think they'll respond next time to make sure you and your family get the best table and a delicious meal? The answer—very quickly. The same goes for practically anyone with whom you employ this tactic. It's one of the best techniques for long-term *Winning Without Intimidation.*

When sending your note, insert the notecard into a number 10 envelope. *Hand-write* the person's name and address and make it a point to *hand-stamp* the envelope, instead of putting it through a postage meter. You want the letter to be opened, not to be perceived as "junk mail." Anyone in the business of mail order will confirm that letters that look personal on the outside increase their odds of being opened tenfold!

Here's an example of how to turn a potential lemon into a lemonade using these notes:

At an annual convention of an association to which I belong, I was sitting at a table with about ten other people. There were several conversations taking place simultaneously around the table, and without realizing it, I was talking a bit louder than I should have been.

A man sitting next to me—an older gentleman and a true center-of-influence within the association—turned to me with a touch of annoyance in his voice and said, "Bob, you seem to have quite an audience there." Although he could have been more tactful in his reproach, his point was made and taken. And he was right.

Upon returning from the convention, I immediately sent him a personal note. Not an apology note, but a thank you note, which read, "Dear Mr. Jones, Thank you. It was a pleasure meeting you at the recent convention. Best of success in the coming year. Regards, Bob."

That was it. Nothing was mentioned about the incident. It was just a simple thank you note. Did it achieve the desired result, which was to take a potentially negative situation and turn it into a positive experience? Well, at the following convention one year later, upon spotting me, he made his way over from across the room to shake hands and greet me like an old friend. A good relationship developed, and he and I are very friendly to this day.

As far as the timing regarding the sending of your

58

note is concerned, my suggestion is to do it right away. In many communities you can mail a letter before midnight and it will arrive locally the very next day. Having it appear on a person's desk at work or in their home the day after they meet you or have performed a service is a very nice touch.

I suggest getting into the habit of immediately sending notes. One major factor that separates those who succeed in any area of life, from those who don't, is the ability to take action at the correct moment. In today's superfast-paced society, that moment is NOW. Actually, *ability* isn't even the correct word. The proper term is *self-discipline*.

Realize the following fact of life: The longer you wait to do what you know you should do now, the greater the odds are that you'll never actually get around to doing it. I call this the Law of Diminishing Intent. Sending notes is too important a tactic to never actually get around to doing.

### It's not negotiable?
### Sure it is.

Earlier, when talking about tactics of negotiation, I mentioned that every time you attempt to get something from someone he originally was not about to give, including cooperation, you're negotiating. Different situations call for different tactics. One situation, or challenge, may be when someone has just a little bit of power, and since that's all he has, he does his best to use it as much as possible in order to satisfy his ego.

In *Winning Without Intimidation*, we'll again put into action the Three P's—Politeness, Patience and Persistence, as well as give that person the power they already have anyway.

I was in Toledo, Ohio, about to speak a few hours later at a sales rally. We were setting up the tables where, after the program, people would have the opportunity to pur-

59

chase my books and tapes. One important aspect of merchandising learning resources after a program such as this is having the tables set up in a prime space. As people exit to the restrooms or the concession stands or to stretch their legs in the hallway, they'll be close enough to the table to remind them of the merchandise for sale. They can see the albums and books, pick them up, etc. Table positioning is very important.

Obviously, the positioning of our table is much more important to my staff and me than it is to the convention arena personnel. Understandably, they just want to see things run smoothly with no major hassles to make them work even harder then they already have to. Upon noticing our table further away from the main door then was beneficial, we had the table moved to a more advantageous spot. Since the space right next to the door was already taken, the spot we chose was against a wall directly opposite the door. This was actually even better. People would be facing us directly whenever they left the main room and would almost bump right into us upon re-entering. I wondered, in fact, why hadn't any of the other speakers, entertainers, or exhibitors thought of that?

I soon found the answer. Mr. Anderson, one of the arena officials, quickly made his way over to our table and informed us we'd have to move. "You can't set up there," he informed us. He was most definitely poised for a knockdown, drag out argument.

I don't blame him. I'm sure he has at least one of those every program held at his arena. A bitter argument ensues and then the person ends up moving, leaving both parties angry and resentful.

He wasn't going to get either of those from me as far as I was concerned; neither an argument nor a moved table. The first step I'd take, as you know by now, is to consciously make the decision to respond, not react. *Respond, not react.*

I extended my hand and said, "I'm Bob Burg." He told

me his name was Scott Anderson. He was just a bit disarmed now and a little nicer when he said, "You're gonna have to remove the table, and set it up down the hall; it's against the rules for a table to be set up here and unfortunately it's non-negotiable."

"Oh, I understand that," I replied.

I continued, respectfully using his title, "Mr. Anderson, what could we do to work out a special arrangement—setting up down the hall will absolutely kill my sales, and I'm wondering if you could use your influence in making a special exception?"

What I just did was to affirm in his mind the fact that I respected him and the power he had. By using the phrase "special exception," I was helping him to think of an answer that he could use *and* take credit for, too.

It wouldn't be quite that easy, however, and patience and persistence would be necessary. He replied, "There is no special exception. As I said, Mr. Burg, there is no negotiating on this."

"Oh, I agree," I replied. I learned the power of agreement from a "gazillionaire" by the name of Tim Foley, a former All-Pro football player with the Miami Dolphins who has made a fortune in the business world—mainly because he has an incredible skill with people, diplomacy being his forte. Rumor has it that Tim reads the book *How to Win Friends and Influence People* every few months in order to keep his skills sharp in that area. I'd say that was good advice. He also works hard, is consistent in his efforts and a real giver of himself to others. That's a recipe for both business and personal success.

"Oh, I agree," I told Mr. Anderson. "Obviously there's a reason for this rule. It must be a protection of some kind, but you know what, I can't figure out what it is—I only know that if I don't have this space I'm in big trouble. I can tell you're the type of person who seeks solutions to challenges—do you have any advice on how we could pull this off?"

61

He was getting a bit flustered now for a couple of reasons: One, I wasn't giving up. That probably isn't strange, I'm sure he's used to exhibitors violently arguing with him for the longest time. The difference is that there's no argument here. Just a very respectful guy—totally respectful—massaging his ego, and gently challenging his wisdom and expertise by asking him to come up with a solution.

"The problem is, Mr. Burg, that with your tables here, it's still too close to the door. With your tapes and books set up before the program starts, people will be crowding around your table to shop. It will make it hard for people wanting to get in and get seats to get past the crowd. That's why, unfortunately, as much as I'd like to help, it's still non-negotiable."

Finally, good news, I thought to myself.

You might be thinking, Bob, are you crazy!?! He just gave you awful news! Nnnoooo, he didn't. He just supplied me with the answer—an answer that would allow him to let us stay there, while emotionally satisfying him and logically giving him the loophole he needed so he wouldn't stop from doing the right thing just for the sake of protecting his ego.

So you know where I'm coming from, remember that he talked about the challenge being people crowding around the table *before* the program, not allowing the rush of people wanting to take their seats to get by. We *never* open our table before the program. We find we do much better by not opening it until I've presented my program on stage. Then, people have more of an interest in checking out the materials, books and tapes at the table. The challenge Mr. Anderson spoke about would never happen. Of course, that's logical, but his ego, like anyone's, wouldn't make decisions based on logic. So I phrased it to him this way:

"Mr. Anderson, you just came up with the answer. I will give you my word that we will not open up the table until *after* I speak on stage. In fact, we'll cover it with the sheets over here and no one will even be able to see anything. You figured out the solution we would need to have, and I can live with not opening my table until after I speak. I'm only concerned about being here after the actual speech."

It worked. He got the credit. I got the solution. We had one of our best sales nights ever. The positioning of the table was about the best I've ever had.

Here's the funny part: In order to save face and his power position even more, he made us agree to one other provision. The next morning, we would have to set up in our original spot. This made absolutely no logical sense. None at all. The only challenge with our being in the spot we wanted was the opening crowd needing to get to their seats, and that had been worked out. But his ego needed that concession from me in front of everyone else, to make sure we all knew he was still the boss.

I knew that tomorrow didn't matter. The majority of business is done immediately after my live presentation. By tomorrow, those who still wanted my materials would find my table 20 yards away. They weren't the ones who needed it right in front of them. So I "grudgingly" agreed and we had our spot.

I figured that by the next morning he would have forgotten all about the final concession, since his point was made. But guess what? The next morning, our table had been moved.

Do people make decisions logically or emotionally?

Remember the Three P's—Politeness, which is also respect, Patience and Persistence. Let that person feel their power, want to help you, and think the solution was theirs. If necessary, concede a minor point to make them feel you didn't totally get what you wanted. Sometimes, losing a little bit of nothing is a very worthwhile trade-off to come out *Winning Without Intimidation*.

**How you ask is more important than what you ask**

Sitting at the Denny's restaurant counter for breakfast, I noticed the waitress possessed one of the most unusual foreign accents I'd ever heard. It was very nice, just different. In fact, I could hear that the couple next to me were trying to figure out its origin—as was I. When the waitress came back over to our general area I said, "Excuse me, that's a lovely accent you have. Where are you originally from?" With a big smile, she thanked me, and mentioned that a lot of people seem to enjoy her accent.

As she walked away, the husband of the couple next to me said to his wife, "Now that's how you ask a person something." I believe he was saying that taking a moment to phrase a question nicely—with kindness and respect—and saying it with the right intonation, makes a big difference in getting what we want and need from people. I simply call it *Winning Without Intimidation*.

You can imagine the special service and attention and smiles I received from the waitress for the remainder of the meal.

A woman named Glenna Salisbury is one of my friends and mentors from the National Speakers Association. She tells a very funny story that truly illustrates the fact that what you say isn't nearly as important as how you say it.

Glenna tells of a young English teacher who had worked hard all year trying to help an Asian transfer student master the English language. Understandably, he was very appreciative.

On the final day of school, the teacher walked into her classroom and on her desk was a single yellow rose. Next to it was a note written by the young man. It read, "Dear Teacher, one day this rose will fade and die, but you will *smell* forever!" The words may not have been exactly right, but do you think she felt insulted or complimented?

64

She was delighted because of the intention.

Here's a little game I learned from Zig Ziglar which demonstrates how *the way* you say something can dramatically alter *what you mean* to say. In this exercise, I want you to accentuate the one word in the sentences below which appears in ***bold-face italics***. Just put extra emphasis on that one word as you read out loud. Each sentence is exactly the same, but watch what happens when you place emphasis on the different words.

***I*** didn't say she stole the money.

I ***didn't*** say she stole the money.

I didn't ***say*** she stole the money.

I didn't say ***she*** stole the money.

I didn't say she ***stole*** the money.

I didn't say she stole the ***money***.

Aren't the differences interesting? All because you merely accentuated a different word in the exact same sentence!

Often, it isn't what we say, but how we say it! Our pets know what we mean by the way, tone and manner we talk to them. So do our children. It's safe to say your customers, prospects, loved ones, friends, and anyone with whom you may need to win over without intimidation can sense the very same thing.

**Smiling equals success**

Read any good book on people skills and there will be at least a mention of the power of a smile. It's also the easiest technique to learn in order to Win Without Intimidation.

Believe it or not, for some people smiling takes a bit of practice. Hey, for some it takes a lot of practice! We're not talking about a smile just to be positive, but to Win Without Intimidation. Regarding the positive aspect though, it's been said, "You don't smile because you're happy—you're happy *because* you smile."

That's true! It's a physiological fact. When you smile, there is a chemical response within the body that actually compels you to feel happy.

Do this: Smile really big, right now, and feel sad . . .

Can't do it—won't work. When you smile, you make yourself happy, improve your attitude, and also improve the other person's attitude and expectations of you.

John Mason, author of *Let Go of Whatever Makes You Stop*, says, "One of the single most powerful things you can do to influence others is to smile at them."

Very true! Dale Carnegie devoted an entire segment of his great book, *How To Win Friends & Influence People*, to this single fact. I use this technique often, and so do most other people used to *Winning Without Intimidation*.

Very few people smile without a particular reason. By smiling, you give yourself a distinct advantage over everyone who is not smiling. Get that sincere smile on your face—and do it before you deal with anybody; the service person, government worker, your boss, the waitperson, your spouse, anybody. Get yourself ready for that person to like you and smile back *at you*!

I employ this simple tactic all the time and everyday with incredible results, and I know others who regularly do the same. They quite often get waited on or helped at a crowded desk first, just because the person sees them with that smile.

We spoke earlier about having to talk to a manager regarding having a challenge with something, or you might have to question somebody about the fact there's an extra charge on your bill. Greet that person with a really nice smile and watch their mind-set match yours. The person who smiles becomes a pleasure to deal with.

Smile . . .

When walking into a restaurant on your way to take your seat, smile at whomever's eyes meet yours. Do that enough and people will notice you. They'll describe *you* as the one with charisma.

I often stop at the local grocery store in the morning to pick up bagels. As I walk up to pay, the cashier, one of the other employees or another patron who's seen me in there before, will comment on the fact that I'm always smiling.

Sometimes they'll even say, "You're the only person I know who's in a good mood in the morning." Once an employee said, "Gee, you're in a good mood today." I responded with a smile, "Have you ever seen me not in a good mood?" He replied, "Actually, no I haven't."

Do you think I get good service and smiles from the employees and other patrons? Sure I do. If I ever needed to approach anyone there for any specific reason, do you think I'd be taken seriously? Absolutely!

This does not mean I am always in a good mood. I have my difficulties, challenges, frustrations, just like everyone else. But that doesn't mean I have to wear it on my face, in public, and spread my bad mood to everybody else.

If I'm depressed or hurting inside, that's nobody else's business. What's that old saying? "Fifty percent of the people don't care that you're feeling badly, and the other half are glad." I'd like to think that's not totally true, but the point is people respond more positively to those who appear to be positive.

The fastest way I know to change my bad feeling is to smile. Remember what I said earlier about how a smile causes the release of neurochemicals into your brain? Those chemicals are called endorphins, and they're the substance responsible for the positive "mood" human beings experience and call joy. That means you can change how you feel by simply smiling. (And notice if *that* makes you smile . . . )

When you smile, people begin talking about you in a positive way. What's the payoff for that?

You'll probably never know until it happens. However, the result both short- and long-term is you've made others feel good and you've contributed positively to your world and the world of others.

Does it work for you in the business world, too?

Sure, because you never know who you're going to meet and who will take notice of you. A smile makes people curious about you—why is he smiling? What makes her so happy? They may ask about what line of work you're in and ask about you personally. I know it's happened to me.

What about on a social level?

This doesn't count if you're married, but I've met several nice women because they noticed me smiling and asked about me. Simply smiling led to introductions I would not otherwise have gotten.

Tim Foley, who I mentioned earlier, and his friend and protégé Bubba Pratt, another hugely successful business person with excellent people skills, are two of the best I've seen when it comes to greeting a person with a smile. My dad has been a master of that very same skill from as early as I can remember. People would see him coming and practically roll out the red carpet, whether it was the first or the 20th time they had seen him. I was always amazed.

You know some people who are like that, don't you? It's sincere! They like people and they show it. Even if you have to work at making it sincere, you can do it. It pays well. Really well!

One of the best examples of the power of a smile I've experienced happened to me years and years ago when I walked into a bank in Tampa, Florida. There was one long line and two shorter lines, and I was wondering why the people in the back of the long line weren't moving to the other lines. As soon as I saw the teller, I understood why. She had the most incredible, radiant, friendly smile I've ever seen—before or since.

That smile was worth waiting in as long a line as it took, just to be waited on by her and get to bask in the glow of that smile one-on-one—even for just a few moments. I'm not usually overly dramatic, but her's was a smile that obviously intoxicated a lot of people in a very positive way. So, I took my place at the end of the line . . . and *I had just come in to ask for directions*!

We like to be around those kinds of people because they make other people feel so darn good! I had to *learn* how to do that, and perhaps you feel you have to learn how as well. It doesn't matter whether or not it comes naturally for you . . . you *can* learn to master this skill—anyone can.

Les Giblin suggests that in the same way voice instructors teach their pupils to breathe deeply and let their voices come from way down low in their bodies, you must do the same with your smile. Instead of smiling from the diaphragm, smile from deep in your heart.

Your smile *must* be genuine or it will come across as manipulative. We've all seen people with that kind of smile.

Practice your smile all the time. As you do this, make yourself feel happy at first by thinking of something very pleasant. The more you practice, the more your friendly, persuasive smile will come across as authentic, natural and *yours*.

### Getting people to give you more

You can easily persuade someone to give you more than she normally would. Simply plant the seeds with the person as she is doing what she'd regularly do.

For instance, imagine you love hot carrots as a vegetable with your meal. You're at a cafeteria and the server is beginning to spoon the carrots onto your plate. You want more than you know she is planning to give you. You've already greeted her with a smile, which sets you apart from everyone else and she's taken notice—she smiled back. As she begins to serve the first spoonful you say, "Umm, thank you, I love those." You'll get more carrots than most people will, even if that person is not usually inclined to break routine.

Tell the mechanic working on your car, "John, you're an *artist*, man, the way you work on these things." People love being called "*artists*" at jobs not usually associated with art. He'll probably give you the best service he's capable of giving.

A friend of mine used to refer to the man making the submarine sandwiches at our favorite sandwich shop as an *artist*, and he was. He loved showing off his artistic sandwich making skills to my friend and me. Of course, that took lots of extra meat and fixings, not to mention extra care and attention.

To the busy woman in the clothing store who's loaded with people wanting her attention: Smile and say, "I can tell you're busy, and I don't want to be a pest, I'll try and take up as little of your time as possible." Chances are you'll get more of her time than will the next 100 people.

### The technique of, "I know that you..."

As people of ego, you and I don't appreciate being told by someone what to say or not to say, what to do or not to do. Even worse is for someone to instruct us in something *we already think we know all about*.

When you need to be sure that a person will come through for you—and not say or do the wrong thing—you must phrase what you say in such a way that he and his ego will not be offended. Tell him that you know that *he already knows*.

Before giving the specific instructions, you might begin with the words, "I know that you...," and then provide him with the necessary information.

70

Here's an example: "Tom, *I know that you* believe in being sensitive to people's feelings; that's why I have no doubt you'll go out of your way to be especially tactful when telling Dave about the mistake he made on that report."

"Rhonda, *I know you already know* that the statistics need to be filed in a three tier set-up. You have a way of always putting these things together correctly."

"Marie, *I know you were going to* stack these here anyway; I just needed to tell you because of my own insecurity."

Saying things that way takes the sting out of it, leaves people feeling good about you—and about *themselves*—and assures that they do in fact *do* what's expected of them.

### The same techniques over and over

My neighbor Carol—a staff supervisor for a local mid-size company—called to invite me to a local dinner theater show. As a holiday bonus, her company had decided to send the entire staff to the theater for a night of fine food and entertainment, and Carol invited me to come along as her guest.

Because the person with the tickets had not yet arrived, the manager would not let us into the main dining area to sit down and begin eating. He politely asked us to wait at the bar. Nursing a soft drink, I waited with the rest of them. Carol, who could be somewhat fiery and argumentative, wasn't about to let it go at that.

She announced to us all that she was not happy. She wanted us to begin eating right away, so that we'd have plenty of time to enjoy our food. As far as Carol was concerned, the manager knew we were simply waiting for the person with the tickets to arrive, so why couldn't we just go in now! Although I happened to have been in agreement with Carol, I was an invited guest and didn't feel it was my place to say anything.

71

Then Carol announced, for all of us to hear, "I'm going to raise a fuss about this!" And she did.

After calling the manager over she began to verbally assault his intelligence, or lack thereof. How do you suppose he reacted? The fact that I used the word "reacted" and not "responded," probably gives you a hint. He argued right along with her.

It went on for several minutes, Carol telling him why he should let us go in and the manager telling us why he couldn't. A totally emotional conversation between two adults not acting as adults. There was Carol, acting the Parent, admonishing the manager as if he were a Child (Remember the Parent, Adult, and Child states we discussed earlier). The manager, feeling scolded, was defensively arguing back.

Seeing that this was not going to end anytime soon and realizing how simple it would be to solve, I waited until the two combatants took a simultaneous breath and said to the manager, "Sir, I totally understand where you're coming from and what the challenge is. In fact, in a similar situation, I might feel the same way. Let me ask, if we were to assume total responsibility for the seating assignments—if I could get the staff supervisor herself to agree that you would be totally off the hook—would you consider letting us go in now?"

He looked at me with a smile, and to everyone's amazement but mine, he said that wouldn't be a problem. I replied, "Great, because being able to eat our meal without having to hurry would certainly add to our enjoyment of the show. By the way, I appreciate your help and understanding." He responded—yes, responded—by saying, "My pleasure."

He then personally escorted us to our seats and checked on our comfort several times throughout the evening. At one point later in the evening, when he noticed that one of the people in our group got up with her camera to take a group picture, he even walked over and offered to take the picture for her, so the woman with the camera could be part of the shot.

Carol was astounded by what took place and asked what my "secret" was. I explained it really wasn't so much a secret as much as a genuine caring for others and finding a win-win solution to a challenge. I'm not sure whether she grasped the concept, or continues to go through her life fighting a never-ending battle. A lot of people do that. The more we share these techniques with others, however, the more, little by little, we can do our part to make this an easier world in which to live.

### Building rapport: a key to *Winning Without Intimidation*

People generally respond well to people who are like them. Having similarities with another person increases your chances of persuading her to go along with your ideas. Often times, however, you are nothing like that other person. The two of you have less in common than a Hatfield and a McCoy.

In those cases you need to really stretch: What do you have in common with that person? Are you both married? Do you both have kids? Do you both have kids about the same age? Are you weekend athletes? Sports fans? Have similar hobbies, pleasures, recreation? Find out through questions.

Geographical sameness can be determined fairly easily, and that's a good start. Ask where she lives. Ask where she grew up. If you both live in Massachusetts, but are originally from Boston, that's a great starting point. You can bring up similar areas you're both familiar with. If you live in Florida, and she lives in Louisiana, but both grew up in different towns in Massachusetts, "Hey, I'm originally from Massachusetts myself!" That's something you can build on in establishing rapport with that person.

You can *really* stretch it. Let's say you live in Florida, and she lives in California. You grew up in Massachusetts, and she grew up in New Jersey, "Hey, I'm from the East Coast, too."

This technique can pretty much be used until you get to the point of, "Hey, I'm from that planet, too." Geographic origins or location, as well as other similarities, can be used as excellent rapport builders.

### Pretend all the other drivers are your next door neighbors

Two concepts I've mentioned often are "politeness," and "responding as opposed to reacting." If you are not used to regularly enlisting these two key techniques, then you'll get caught often in what I call "the heat of the moment." That's when the challenge with another person occurs and, because the right way of handling the situation is not internalized in our minds and our hearts, we slip up and lose control. The situation—and often the other person—ends up controlling you, instead of you controlling the situation.

Here's an exercise that will serve as excellent practice in mastering politeness and responding, two very important skills in *Winning Without Intimidation.*

Ever notice when you're in a car, the other drivers seem to take liberties they might not take if they were not under the protection of a moving vehicle? People are rude. They'll butt up in line. They'll cut you off. They'll even give you the "I'm Number One" sign with the incorrect finger in the air.

In his book *If Life is a Balancing Act, Why Am I So Darn Clumsy?*, Dick Biggs suggests pretending that all the other drivers are your next door neighbors. Use that great idea in working on your skills of politeness and responding. Every time that another driver is rude in any way—no matter how much you have to fight yourself at first—*respond* by being polite.

Use either a wave or a smile, or nod your head in

acknowledgment—or even put your hand up as if to say, "Sorry, my fault." You can also let a driver go first at an intersection, or let them cut in front of you from another lane.

You'll be amazed at how many people will be friendly in return—which is a good feeling. You'll turn a potential enemy into a friend. You'll develop your skills of politeness, and responding *instead* of reacting, in record time. That's an all around win!

By pretending that all the other drivers on the road are your next door neighbors, you'll begin internalizing for later action these very important skills for *Winning Without Intimidation.*

### One result of being impolite
The following example will probably happen only rarely, but people who succeed usually base their success on those little differences which are not noticed and acted on by the masses of average, less successful people.

One afternoon as I was walking out my office door, I crossed paths with a young, sharply-dressed man. I politely smiled and said, "Hello," as I would to anybody, yet he responded with what I call a "don't bother me, buddy" look. Obviously he figured I was *just* another salesperson or one of my company's employees. He probably didn't guess I was "the company." When I got to my car I called Ilene, my office manager, and asked who that was.

She explained that he was the guy we were buying the two new computers from and that he was outside her office now waiting for her. I told her what happened and said I'd rather not buy from him, and that if she'd like, I'd come in and tell him personally so she wouldn't have to. Surprisingly, she told me she would be glad to handle that, because he had been rude to her on the phone the last time he called.

He had called to ask for directions and she picked up the phone instead of the receptionist. He was quick and

75

hurried while she was providing the directions to him, and as soon as she finished, he abruptly hung up without saying "Thank you." I'm guessing he thought it was okay to act that way to a secretary or receptionist.

That young man lost two nice, easy sales . . . about $5000 worth. He had simply come in with the paperwork for us to endorse. We had ordered those computers over the phone. That situation is what some people in the selling profession call a "laydown." That sale couldn't have been any easier for him. He had to really work at losing that one . . . and he did.

I guess you could say it's a good idea to be polite to everyone you meet. Not only is it the best and proper way to act, but you don't always know who you're talking to.

As a kicker to this story, several months later I found out that an acquaintance of mine had gone to work as manager of that computer store. I related what happened and he was not at all surprised. He explained that the three salespeople they had when he started—the guy from the previous story being one—had created a whole bunch of ill will for the company by treating practically all their prospects and customers in a similar way.

They were all let go . . . all fired when the owners heard enough of the negative feedback from customers (and probably *former* customers). My acquaintance added that he and a couple others had been brought in by the ownership to restore the goodwill that had once been an integral part of their company.

Crazy, isn't it?

### Politeness, respect, and the implied threat
After days of not having our repeated calls returned by our sales representative, my Office Manager took the only reasonable course of action she could and called the man's boss to ask why that was. Ilene handled this perfectly, first letting the boss know that we've always been pleased with their company and the excellent service

76

they've provided to that point. We soon received a call from the sales rep, Gary, who had just taken over the area, and he was understandably not at all happy to have been "told on." He and I had never met before, but he asked to speak with me. I was happy to take his call. "Good morning, Gary."

Gary began with a really defensive edge to his voice. "Why did you call my boss instead of calling me directly?"

"Unfortunately, Gary, we've had a challenge with our equipment for the past couple of days. We called you several times, and, surprisingly, didn't hear back from you."

Gary replied, "I just took over this territory and I have other customers. I can't get back to everybody right away."

I responded, "I appreciate that. I know you're very busy, but a call of acknowledgment would have made us feel a lot better and then we could have scheduled an appointment for you to come in."

Despite my politeness and respect, he still wasn't grasping the idea. He again replied that he was busy and could only return calls in order after the jobs were done.

Now came what you've heard me refer to as "The nice but *implied* threat."

"Gary, I understand where you're coming from and sense that right now, you're feeling a lot of pressure from people within your new territory. Here's where I am: We need to know we can be serviced by whatever company we choose to do our business with. I'd like it to remain yours. You and I will obviously have to work according to each others needs and expectations, and if we can't, we'll both have to do what will be best for our individual situations."

He understood.

You know what I was doing without an explanation— establishing a foundation of politeness and respect. I then built our position in the sales representative's mind as a customer worth fighting for.

Remember, people deal with ranters and ravers and screamers all day long. If they are going to have to sacrifice one of them or a customer who is polite and respectful, which one do you think it will be?

When courtesy alone didn't get through to Gary, it was time for *the nice but implied threat*. It was effective in letting him know not to confuse my niceness with weakness. The implied threat is so effective because it clearly shows the other person credibility and seriousness of purpose, yet it doesn't paint him into a corner from which he can't escape without his ego screaming in pain.

Someone not versed in the purpose of *Winning Without Intimidation* may wonder why I went through all that trouble instead of just changing companies and going with someone new. Let's take a look at the result of my conversation with Gary.

Gary began popping in to check on us whenever he was in the area. One time, when we were short-handed and had to process a bunch of orders—which had nothing to do with *his* company—Gary actually insisted on staying and helping us. Unbelievable! I think Gary paid us so much attention because we were probably one of the only customers that treated *him* so well.

What if I had just changed companies? Who knows how *their* rep would have treated us. Or the next, or the next. Eventually, we might have even gotten back around to Gary's company, and we'd have had zero credibility, since we'd be doing business with them out of weakness, not strength. How about all the lost time for set-up and the expense it would have taken to switch companies? No, the best way is to handle it right the first time. That is truly *Winning Without Intimidation*!

**Don't try to teach a pig to sing**
Is there ever a time when *Winning Without Intimidation* won't work? Yes, there is. "When is that?" you ask. Let me explain it this way.

I once heard the saying, "Don't try to teach a pig to sing. It will just frustrate you—and really annoy the pig!"

You could also use, "Don't ever argue—or attempt to Win Without Intimidation—with a crazy person."

When I use the word "crazy," I'm not talking about people who have a medically determined condition beyond their control. I'm talking about people who have taken on an entire personality of disagreeableness or have a particular—and usually particularly negative—attitude about something.

These are the people, who, for whatever reason, just aren't going to work with you, me or anyone else. Their emotional state has predetermined the facts and their mind cannot be opened through logic nor emotion. Don't confuse *them* with the facts. They feel wronged by someone or something, and they're giving back as good as they got!

These people often have no idea that's what they're doing. They all seem to believe they are the most understanding, open-minded people in the world.

They're not, but neither you nor I can change their minds.

We all know at least one of these people, and as much as it goes against every grain of our thinking, we need to let them go and do their own thing. That's only a very last resort, of course, but it's one of those rare times when we say, "NEXT!" If you try to Win Without Intimidation with these people, you'll only frustrate yourself and annoy them.

**Pre-apology approach**

As I was walking up to the ticket counter, the agent did not look happy. He looked downright miserable. I needed him to be working *with* me, because I was going to have to change a couple of items on my ticket. But this was a man who was prepared to be difficult. How do you work effectively with that potential challenge and end up *Winning Without Intimidation*?

Approach with the smile discussed earlier. This had no

79

effect on my agent. I have to admit, at that point, I really felt like telling him to shape up and get with it. But that would have just turned a potential enemy into a *real* enemy. Instead, I disarmed him by using the "Pre-apology" approach. That's where you apologize in advance for all he is going to do for you.

"I'm sorry you've got to bother with all this stuff, it must be a real pain in the neck."

That was it. It was that simple. From there he went above and beyond for me. All he needed was for someone to understand what he was feeling. Can you believe it? With that one small statement, his attitude completely changed for the better. I'll bet he was friendlier for the customers following me, too.

The natural *reaction* would've been to match his scowl and battle to an eventual lose/lose. My associate, who was with me at the counter, compared me to her former boss who, she said, would have screamed and yelled and maybe gotten his way and maybe not, but would've definitely ruined the moment and quite possibly the day for everyone involved.

Remember Simeon ben Zoma's saying, "A mighty person is one who can control their emotions and make of an enemy a friend."

### What, who, and how

While reading a very good book by Milo O. Frank, entitled *How To Get Your Point Across In 30 Seconds or Less*, I was reminded that there are three essentials for every form of spoken or written communication: "Know *what* you want, know *who* can give it to you, and know *how* to get it."

Know exactly *what* it is you want from the transaction with the other person. Focus your efforts on an outcome you'll be happy with.

Know *who* can give it to you. Do you need to find a tactful way of getting from the person you're with to the person who really has the power to say "Yes?" Nearly anyone on any level can say "No." You need to know who it is who can give you what you want.

You accomplish the *how* part by using the skills and techniques in this book and those you learn from other sources as well.

### Find the who

In a recent issue of *Selling* magazine, I read about Joe Cousineau, president of his own company in the oil business. He expertly used the art of finding the "who" when he was regional sales manager for another company within the industry.

Cousineau was trying to land an account with the largest purchaser in his region—a company already doing huge business with his competitor. He arrived right on time for his meeting with the purchasing agent, but was then distressed by the treatment he received.

The purchasing agent did not invite Joe to come in to make his presentation, but instead, while standing in the lobby and looking at his watch, told him he had exactly five minutes to explain why the company should change over to Joe's product, instead of staying with the supplier already in use.

Joe knew that five minutes was far from enough time, and to make matters worse, the purchasing agent never made eye contact, showed no interest in what Joe was saying, and would check the time every 30 seconds. At the end of five minutes, the purchasing agent abruptly stopped the presentation, announced time was up, shook Joe's hand, turned on his heel and left.

Joe was stunned. The receptionist, who witnessed this transaction, was quite embarrassed by her boss' behavior but was not in a position to do anything about it. Joe left.

Had he not been taken by surprise, and hundreds of miles from home, Cousineau probably wouldn't even have given a presentation. He would have most likely questioned the purchasing agent on how they could work out a better time to meet in a more efficient setting. In fact, he may have done just that.

What I do know is that the way Joe Cousineau handled the situation from there on was a textbook example of finding the "who" and then *Winning Without Intimidation*.

After reassessing the situation back in his own office, Joe realized that he did not deserve that kind of treatment. It would also be wrong to let that purchasing agent's rude, unprofessional attitude keep his company from realizing the benefits of Cousineau's products.

Joe determined that the "who" to talk to was the president of the company, and that's who he called. Joe explained to the president that his product had been proven to be superior and outperform its competition at far better terms and prices, and that he had arranged a meeting earlier in the week with the company's purchasing agent to review those points.

Then he calmly explained to the president what had transpired and told him that the purchasing agent's conduct . . . now this is a great word . . . *confused* him. What an excellent choice of words, putting the onus of the misunderstanding upon himself—a great "I message"—which you *know* piqued the president's curiosity.

Joe continued by saying that he had decided, before "closing the books" on this company altogether, to break the usual chain of command and phone the president directly.

Joe told the president he was new in the territory, and asked if it was company policy to give vendors only five minutes in the lobby for presentations. If not, did they have a special arrangement with another supplier, and was that possibly the reason for his unusual treatment?

"Was the purpose to discourage me?" Joe phrased that question carefully enough to not imply any improprieties between the company and their present supplier.

The president asked Joe to describe again precisely what happened and if there were any witnesses. After learning about the receptionist, the president confirmed Joe's story, apologized and gave Joe an appointment with him personally, without the purchasing agent present.

Cousineau put together a transaction which to this day ranks as that division's third-largest account ever. It was also the sale which Cousineau credits for turning his career around. As for the purchasing agent, management decided to put him into sales, so he would learn what it's like to get the sort of mistreatment he had been dispensing to others.

Joe Cousineau's story provides an excellent example of finding the "who," putting that person on your side, and then expertly *Winning Without Intimidation.*

### How to politely end a telephone conversation

When someone, maybe even a close friend or associate, is constantly calling or keeping you on the phone, how do you end the conversation politely and effectively, without offending that person? Here's what works for me and for others: Begin the conversation with, "Hey, great to hear from you, I'm just about to . . . (step out, meet with a client, move on to a phone appointment, etc.), but I've got about 30 seconds, what's going on?"

Usually the person will not be sensitive or aware enough to end in 30 seconds, even though you've tactfully told him. Wait until he finishes his most recent point, then talk. Say two or three words and cut *yourself* off by saying, "Oh, I forgot. Gotta run (to my call, meeting, lobotomy—whatever). Nice talking with you, though. We'll talk again soon."

That will set you free.

## Making the best out of being around someone you don't like

Hey, we're all human, and because we are—human I mean—there are certain people you and I genuinely don't like being around. It happens! A person may be just the type whose personality style gets on your nerves—grates on you. But what about when you're in a situation where you have to be around that person, such as work or some special project? Perhaps the worst case of all—this guy you don't like is related to someone close to you, maybe your best friend's or your boss's husband?

The best way to handle the situation is to work on helping that other person adjust their ways of doing certain things. Train them, without their realizing they're being trained, to do things in a more positive and likeable way.

Just make a game out of it. Not at their expense, mind you; have fun with them—the two of you *together*. Catch them doing something right or even make up something you wish they would do right and compliment them on doing it. Build on small successes. They'll begin to continue doing those things they get verbally rewarded for. Whether positive or negative, "Behavior that gets rewarded—gets repeated."

This leads into another area of *Winning Without Intimidation* which is called edification.

### Edification

To edify, according to one of the meanings in *Webster's*, is to *build*. When you edify a person, you literally build them up in the minds of other people and, perhaps most importantly, in their own mind, too.

Edify a person, to others and to themselves, even for the things you *wish* they would do. They'll soon begin to "believe their own press," and start adopting the traits and behaviors for which they are being edified.

"Jim sure is precise in the way he fills out his reports."

"Mary, I love how you always handle people with such perfect tact."

"My spouse is the most supportive partner in the world."

"Dave, one thing about you—you may be direct, but you are always fair."

When in doubt as to what to say *about* someone or *to* someone—*edify*!

### Resolving conflict to make-up without intimidation

One of the most difficult challenges for human beings is resolving conflicts with one another. There will be times of anger and frustration between others and ourselves no matter what the relationship—friend, spouse, parent, child, co-worker. It's one of the things that happen even when we do our best to avoid it. How do we resolve these conflicts and redevelop our relationship with the other person? How do we return to speaking terms and mutual enjoyment?

Dr. Paul W. Swets, author of the wonderful book *The Art of Talking so that People Will Listen*, discusses what he calls "Conflict Resolution." According to Dr. Swets, "Once discord has set in, talk is difficult. In fact, discord may have resulted from talk—sharing hostile feelings or dogmatic opinions. Yet talk also can be the best remedy when it is directed by four distinct purposes and their corresponding messages."

The four purposes and their respective messages are:

| Purpose | Message |
| --- | --- |
| 1. Define the problem | "I hear" |
| 2. Look for agreement | "I agree" |
| 3. Understand feelings | "I understand" |
| 4. State views calmly | "I think" |

Dr. Swets explains that we need to first identify the

problem or challenge. Are you sure that both of you are upset about the same thing? Many of us have found ourselves involved in a conflict with someone only to later realize that it was simply, literally a misunderstanding.

"She thought I said this, but what I really meant was ..."

That's why Dr. Swets' corresponding message to defining the problem is "I hear." "What I hear you saying is ...". Dr. Swets suggests making sure that you have stated the point to the other's satisfaction before moving on to the next step.

That next step is to look for agreement. Find something within your challenge upon which you both agree. Take it on yourself to proactively find that point of agreement with the other person. Express the message "I agree." "I agree that I said some unkind things."

As mentioned earlier in the book, finding agreement with the other person's viewpoint will lessen their defense mechanism. They will find the situation less threatening and be more inclined to see your point. Once there is agreement, the foundation is established for the third step.

Step three is understanding the other person's feelings. We've covered the fact that everyone likes to be understood. Dr. Swets would say, "I understand that you might feel ..." completing the sentence with a word that describes what you think the other person is feeling. Dr. Swets provides a list of words to fit various situations:

| afraid | angry | anxious | confident |
| defensive | depressed | happy | hurt |
| troubled | uncertain | upset | worried |

The good news is that even just giving the message that you understand is a positive step. It shows the other person that you *want* to understand. According to Dr. Swets, "If you misinterpret the correct feeling, [the person] will tell you. When you state it accurately, you establish one additional powerful source for dissolving discord, because most people desperately want to be understood at the level of their feelings."

The fourth and final step is to state your views calmly and follow with the corresponding message. Start with "I think ... " or "The way I see it is ... " Complete the sentence with your opinion. Dr. Swets suggests doing this as calmly and briefly as possible. His example is, "I think that you ignored our prior agreement." Another message might be, "I think we need to keep our lines of communication open."

Dr. Swets makes one point in particular which truly fits the philosophies of *Winning Without Intimidation*. "When the Conflict Resolution model is employed, the focus of the controversy gradually changes from attacking one another to attacking a mutual problem and solving it."

I appreciate the wisdom Dr. Swets has shared in his book and find myself rereading it constantly. I highly recommend you add it to your positive persuasion tool kit.

### The One Minute Manager knows

If you have ever read *The One Minute Manager*, by Drs. Ken Blanchard and Spencer Johnson, you'll remember that one of their most famous pieces of advice for managers in effectively dealing with their employees was, "Catch them in the act of doing something right."

When you catch someone in the act of doing the right thing, make sure you verbally acknowledge it and them, and, if appropriate, make sure everyone else in the office or home—or whatever the circumstance may be—knows about the recognition as well. Isn't it great to catch a child in the act of doing something right, and verbally reward her for that?

When the customer service person handles the person in front of you with patience and consideration, make sure you let them know you noticed, and how impressed with them you are. If there are others around, it wouldn't hurt to lavish your praise in a voice loud enough for them to hear, as well.

Once again, whether positive or negative, behavior that gets rewarded gets repeated.

### How to write a request to get action and get what you want

People are not always quick to take the action necessary to live up to their responsibilities. At one time or another, we've all had to chase people for money they owed us and promised to pay, or something similar. Others don't plan to pay at all. You write a nice letter of request. It doesn't get answered. You write another. Again no answer. You begin to write more sternly, then threateningly, and it goes downhill from there.

It's actually much easier and more cost effective to write one letter that gets the results you want. In the following scenario I'll show you just one example. There are many.

I believe the idea will come through as to what really seems to work. Not that it will work every time and with every person. Some people are just the type who live life by not fulfilling their obligations. Typically, this *will* work if the person has even a fair amount of pride, self-respect and humanity. In this example of *Winning Without Intimidation*, I'm going to play upon that sense of pride, self-respect and humanity—*totally*.

I had shot a commercial for a production company, and that evening I discovered that sometime during the day of taping, a suit, two shirts and several of my ties mysteriously "disappeared." There was a slight chance that the other spokesperson involved had taken them by mistake, which could easily be found out, but the odds of that were slim.

The company and I disagreed on whose responsibility it was to protect my suits from being "borrowed forever." After some discussion, we agreed that if the other spokesperson did not have them, the company and I would each assume half the responsibility. They would send me a check for half the amount of the clothes right away.

The person who was my liaison to the owners seemed to be slow in sending the money. I had hoped to do further business with that company, so I didn't want to offend them by nagging for payment.

But after a couple of months, my feelings began to change. My liaison wasn't returning my calls, and that really bothered me. Not returning my phone calls is a sure way to get my goat. To me, it's a sign of disrespect and outright negative acknowledgment. The issue truly wasn't the money. Suits can be replaced. As corny as this may sound to you, it was, in fact, the principle of the thing. They are a good company, comprised of people I very much enjoyed knowing and working with, and I felt they had reneged on a promise. Maybe this is my "old fashioned" thinking, but a promise IS a promise.

I sent the following letter which I believe incorporates many of the principles we've discussed thus far in the book. It focuses on respect for the other person and allowing them to do the right thing while saving face. (So that the company involved in this example cannot possibly be recognized, I've altered the facts and names. The content, however, is totally representative of the situation and my letter.)

Dear Mr. Renfro,

It was a pleasure meeting you during the commercials we did for _____. I appreciate the opportunity to work with your company and the professionalism your company exhibited.

It is with regret that I must bring up an issue that I would have hoped to have been resolved months ago, and I won't assume you are even aware of the situation. May I explain?

On the evening of our shoot it was discovered that one of my suits, two shirts and several ties had been inadvertently taken by someone during the day's taping. There was an extra suit left, however, which we assumed belonged to Mr. Ken Matlin, the other spokesperson. John, my liaison, and I thought that possibly Ken mistakenly took my suit and left me with his, as he had to leave in a hurry during the afternoon to catch a flight. I promised to send the suit to Ken, which I did immediately upon returning to Florida. Unfortunately, Ken did not have my suit, so no one ever found out what happened.

Although over the following months I often reminded John of this challenge, he was vague in his response as to my requests for payment. Throughout the planning and taping of the commercial, John had been wonderful to work with, a true professional, so I'm sure that the vagueness of his responses was because, despite trying diligently, he had not been able to coordinate all parties necessary.

I reminded John several times that I would be willing to go 50/50 on the reimbursement from your company. (Although I don't feel that guarding my clothes during taping should have been my responsibility, I was still willing to split the cost.)

Unfortunately, although I have continued to leave messages both on his voice mail and with Diane, his assistant, I'm now finding that to my surprise, John is not even returning my calls.

Can we work this challenge out to our mutual satisfaction? I hope you feel, as do I, that the best situation is that of the win/win variety. I will hope to hear from you soon. Please feel free to call me at 1-800-726-3667 or fax me at (561)575-2304.

Thank You for your consideration.


Bob Burg

If you enjoyed the way that was handled, you might want to read the letter several more times. Please note how his company was complimented, his sense of fair play and honor was pointed out generously, yet, what I wanted from them is clear. Even John the liaison, who really is a good guy, was treated very well, although I definitely let the boss know about his not returning my calls. That really is a big bugaboo with me.

How did the letter work?

The very next day, at 10:30 AM, Federal Express delivered my check.

### Handling threats by phone and clearing up credit challenges

Several years ago, a woman who was working for me related a challenge she was having. Apparently, the owners of a start-up company she went to work for a year or so earlier had asked her to put her name on their cellular phone application. Although most of us would wonder why an employer would make such a request, and immediately suspect something wrong, Sue, in good faith, did them this courtesy.

As you might expect, they turned out to be less-than-honorable people, and when they went out of business soon after, they left her stuck with about a $1500 phone bill. Sue explained the situation to the cellular phone company, but they insisted that the responsibility for the phone bill was hers and hers alone. They were not concerned at all about the men who owned the company who did not honor their obligation. In other words, it wasn't their problem. Knowing her as I did, I could easily believe that she did not make that story up.

Over the course of the year she would get bills and pay as much as she could. She was not in great shape financially, however, and soon began getting collection letters from the phone company. Finally, a man claiming to be the head of collections called and "urged" her to pay the

91

bill in full or he would have the local sheriff subpoena her to appear in court. According to this man, she would then have to explain to the judge why she wasn't honoring her debt.

Knowing my feeling for winning without intimidation, Sue asked me to help her out, which I was only too glad to do. First, I called the company to see if a simple explanation of the predicament might be enough to have them "call off the dogs." Although the service woman with whom I spoke was very understanding and sympathetic— she explained that many secretaries seem to get victimized by that same scam—there was nothing she could do about it and the bill would have to be paid. Apparently, the man who called Sue earlier was the man who made that decision. I thanked her very much for her time and understanding and asked to speak to "Mr. Gregory."

I introduced myself as Sue's employer and explained that she was a victim. Would the company he worked for be willing to write this off or even reduce her debt? Well, he came on a little strong with me, of course, because that's just how he's used to operating. He said he would need all the money now or he would send the sheriff of our county to visit Sue with the subpoena. I guess the sheriff thing is his usual vehicle of threat.

I replied, "I appreciate your wanting to bring this to closure right away. Since Sue doesn't have the money and you know you can't get blood from a stone, why don't we do this: I will write you out a company check for $400 if, at that point, you'll drop the entire issue. Naturally, I need to have a signed letter from you stating that to be our agreement."

As you already know, what I was doing was, with politeness and respect, establishing with him that he was now dealing with someone he wasn't going to be able to bully, but someone who would still work with him. (After all, I didn't blame the company for wanting their money— and I was even willing to help out in order to get Sue off

92

the hook). His initial threat and tone I just ignored. Many people would have reacted to that, but that would have accomplished nothing. I would let my actions help win without intimidation.

The $400 I offered him was way below what he would be willing to settle for, and I knew that, but I wanted to see where he was. One rule of negotiation is to shoot as low as you can because, first of all, you never know, you just might get it. Secondly, he might come back with another offer. And, if he'll come down once, there's a really good shot he'll come down again. He said, "If you'll make it $1200 and send me a certified check, we'll call it even."

I replied, "Oh, thank you for the offer, I appreciate it . . . unfortunately I'd have to decline that because it's still way too much money. In fact, I know that you know Sue was coerced into putting her name on the agreement even though it was her company who took the service. Her former employer apparently has some challenge with ethics. Maybe you should go after him; it might be a little easier to collect the money from him."

Mr. Gregory replied, "That's not our policy." I responded by saying, "I appreciate that. You know, Mr. Gregory, it's not my policy to pay even a portion of my secretary's former employer's cellular phone bills either, but I'll stretch a bit if you will. I'll tell you what; let me think on this for a day and I'll call you back tomorrow. Thank you so much for your time, I know you want to work this out to everyone's benefit and I appreciate that."

I called my lawyer and asked him what to expect. He told me this guy was "no different from any other collections person and would bully whomever was easiest." Note: certainly not every collections professional does this. Unfortunately, because of those who do, the industry has been saddled with that reputation. Most collection agencies adhere to proper guidelines and go about their job in a legal and ethical manner. He probably could get the money, but he'd have to decide if the effort and money involved was worth it. Also the time, since he was more than three hours outside of our county.

Mr. Gregory called before I did, but he asked to speak to Sue. The receptionist had been instructed to transfer his call to me if that happened (call it a hunch) and I answered, ignoring his indiscretion. "Hi Mr. Gregory, Bob Burg, how are you?"

"Uh, fine Mr. Burg. I came up with a decision. Send me a check for $900 and we'll close this account." I'm thinking, where did this guy come up with the figure $900? A better tactic would have been something like $937. A number such as that gives the perception of a specific reason, that calculations of various costs and other factors had to have been involved. An even number like $900 suggests it was a number grabbed out of thin air. It didn't matter now, though. He should have taken my original offer of $400, which *was* a number grabbed out of thin air.

"Mr. Gregory, again, thank you so much for your time. I appreciate your win/win attitude. Here's what I think we should do." Now, let's pause so I can explain that what I'm going to do right here is a combination of my technique, which I call the implied threat, and a very common negotiating technique called the "higher authority."

You've heard me use the implied threat before. That's when we very nicely, without painting the person into a defensive corner where his ego is at stake, let him know that if he doesn't give in to what we're asking for, his life won't be made any easier. An example of this might be (in a pleasant, sincere voice), "Bill, I've enjoyed doing business with you for so long and would like to continue to do so—I'd hate to feel as though my business isn't worth the extra whatchamacallit I'm asking for." Again, you didn't actually threaten, but your intent was made clear, albeit very nicely.

With the "Higher Authority" technique, you give up

94

your power or authority to make the final decision to someone else; either someone of a higher position in your company, family, etc., or someone of greater knowledge. For instance, "I can't possibly make a decision on that without consulting with my lawyer." Or, "let me run your offer past my (wife, brother-in-law, business partner, choose anyone else you can think of) and I'll let you know."

There are several benefits of this technique—one being that you can always come back with another offer without coming off as the bad guy. Not to mention, the person with whom you're negotiating is put in a position of never exactly knowing where your side stands. Back to our conversation with Mr. Gregory, let's hear how the combination of these techniques sounds.

"Mr. Gregory, again, thank you so much for your time. I appreciate your win/win attitude. Here's what I think we should do. After consulting with my company lawyer, who certainly knows a lot more about the law than I do, he suggested very strongly my not paying any of this bill, and suggested the same for Sue. You represent a fine company with an excellent reputation. The fact is, we all know that the people who ran up the bill should be the people responsible for paying the bill. Here's what I will do for you:

"I'll give you my lawyer's phone number. He said he'll be delighted to speak with you. Unfortunately, Mr. Gregory, he doesn't have the win/win attitude you and I do. He's one of these guys who'd rather fight than work things out as gentlemen as you and I believe in doing. Man, I've seen him tie things up, write letters to company presidents, better business bureaus, newspapers,etc.

"Frankly, he can be a real pain. But you might enjoy speaking with him and finding out where he stands on this issue. I'll call him for you if you like and ask him to call you right now." Mr. Gregory told me that wouldn't be necessary—he'd get with him himself if he felt he needed to.

Sue received a letter from the company shortly after

informing her that the approximately $1500 she owed had been removed from their computers. Folks, these techniques, if applied correctly and persistently, will come through for you more times than not. Frankly, I'd have been more than willing to pay the $400 I originally offered just to help out Sue, but instead, we really ended up *Winning Without Intimidation.*

### *Winning Without Intimidation* by making-up

There are times you might need to break the chain of command to get to the person who can make a major purchase of your products. Your successful sale may make your first contact resentful.

It still behooves you to befriend that first person, because she could still play an important role in your relationship with that company. Letting a person save face after you've gone over her head—and won—can play a major role in how smoothly your relationship with this new client or customer will proceed. The next time you see or talk to her, thank her for her help or contribution in getting the sale.

"Frank, I really appreciate your help," or, "Mary, I appreciate your support and look forward to working with you over the next few months." That's all you need to say.

I know, she had absolutely nothing to do with it. You're right. She knows that. You know that. And she *knows* that you know that. By letting her save face, however, you are showing your class, protecting her ego, and giving her good reason to work harder to help you from that point on.

In my experience, that person will be on your side with loyalty that's truly an asset.

The only instance in which this will not work goes back to what we spoke of earlier, "You can't argue with a crazy person." If he is irrational and totally offended by your actions, he probably won't come over to your side—at least not right away. You'll just have to make sure your other relationships within that organization are even stronger so there's no way sabotage can come into play.

Usually that will not be a challenge. Letting that person save face after you've gone over their head and won will generally bring them over to your side.

### Save money with the Eight Magic Words for *Winning Without Intimidation*

I had changed my flight on the phone the night before. The person on the phone assured me that I wouldn't have to pay the additional $50 to change the tickets, but the woman at the counter the next morning told a different story. I didn't want to react by arguing, yelling and intimidating. I needed to respond by staying cool and thinking before I spoke.

I *admitted*, "I'm sure I misunderstood; the person on the phone was very helpful. Although she did assure me I wouldn't be charged that money, I realize it's put you in a difficult spot, and I apologize for that." Upon hearing that, the agent at the counter started to relax, become more friendly.

Then I said the Eight Magic Words that will generally prompt a person to try their darndest to help you. "If you can't do it, I'll definitely understand." I followed with, "If you can, I'd certainly appreciate it." If it's appropriate, you can add the words, "I don't want you to get yourself in hot water over it."

After checking her computer, she responded, "I'll do it this time."

Treat people with proper respect. Understand their concerns and challenges. Make the request to let them know what you want them to do. Use the eight magic words: "If you can't do it, I'll definitely understand." Win Without Intimidation.

A desk agent at my local airport always tries to wait on me, because he knows with me he's always in a safe place. He's with a person who shows respect and seems to understand what he's going through.

Not surprisingly, *he* ALWAYS comes through for me.

### Back to the implied (but nice) threat

There are times we need to let the person know we mean business and aim to be satisfied in our quest for whatever it is we need or want.

I was speaking at a sales rally on my main topic, Business Networking, and as an introduction to some of these techniques, I explained the concept of *Winning Without Intimidation.* The very next day, someone from the rally gave me the following account:

Mr. and Mrs. Michelson had a small amount of jewelry taken from their hotel room. When they called the manager, he was at first standoffish and said, "Just file a report." The victim, who had just attended my seminar, very calmly replied, "You know, I could do that, and I thank you for your suggestion. Actually, I was really hoping to leave your hotel's name out of it. I'm part of a 2000 person convention and we're supposed to report anything like this to our meeting planner. It really makes me uncomfortable to bring your hotel's name up because, until now, we've really enjoyed our stay."

Although I don't know all the particulars involved, I do know that the manager, from that point on, took it upon himself to be a part of the solution—instead of the problem—and that Mr. and Mrs. Michelson were not charged for their room.

They did the right thing again by expressing their appreciation to the manager for his help and consideration and letting him know that they'd be delighted to share the story of his *helping attitude* with the meeting planner.

Isn't that an excellent example of *Winning Without Intimidation?*

### Getting out of a ticket

Have you ever been pulled over by the police? It can

98

sure be scary. Oh, no! Do I have my drivers license? Is my insurance up to date? How much is this thing going to cost? Will I have to go to traffic school?

Whatever the reason, being pulled over by the flashing blue lights can legitimately shake anyone up. There are three different ways I've noticed people handle this situation.

Some bad mouth and insult the police officer. I'm always amazed when I see this happening. That action will most definitely result in getting the ticket, if not landing a person in jail as well—and certainly not having that officer on your side should their help ever be needed in the future.

Others don't say a word and simply accept the ticket.

A third option is to do your very best at *Winning Without Intimidation* to get out of being given the ticket. I choose option number three.

Let's say you've been pulled over for speeding. I learned a few things from a client of mine named Bernie Marble, who used to be a police officer before going into business for himself and becoming very financially successful. He told us that upon bringing the car to a stop, turn on the inside light (if at night) and place your hands on the steering wheel at the 10:00/2:00 position. Do not make any sudden moves or get out of the car.

The biggest fear a police officer has is that the driver will draw their gun and shoot while the officer is approaching the vehicle. With the inside light on and you in the correct position, the officer can see that you're not a threat and you're showing the proper respect. You're making his job easier.

When the officer asks for your license and registration, a simple "Yes sir," or "Yes ma'am," is a great start.

The officer will probably ask if you realize you were speeding. He or she might even volunteer something like, "I clocked you at 78 in a 65 mph zone."

The best thing is not to make excuses, but instead to

admit fault. "Officer, I totally believe I was going that fast even though I didn't realize it until I saw your lights. I have no excuse. As much as I just hate to get a ticket, I am at fault."

In using this approach, you've just done the best possible job of presenting your case to the officer. You *are* guilty. You know it and the police officer knows it. They've heard more excuses than a sixth grade teacher has about why Bobby didn't have his homework—*again*. By being honest, you have just increased the odds that the officer doesn't really *want* to give you a ticket.

If, at this point, you still feel you need to persuade just a bit more, you might say, "Officer, I'm definitely in the wrong. This isn't something I usually do, and I'm wondering if there's any chance of not getting a ticket, or maybe just a warning. If you can't do it, I'll definitely understand."

You've done everything right, showed total respect, and if he can now justify the situation in his own mind, there's a good chance you won't get a ticket. This won't work every time; it will work some of the time.

It's worked for me when my foot's been just a bit heavy on the pedal or I didn't come to a complete stop at a stop sign, and it's worked for many others. I'm not recommending you do any of these things. They are illegal and wrong, and I know at times I don't drive as carefully as I should. I still don't want to get a ticket, and this technique has worked for me.

One time, though, the officer—a really nice guy—told me that as much as he appreciated my attitude, he never goes back on giving someone a ticket if they're in the wrong. I was in the wrong. He gave me a ticket. At least he was honest and I almost felt good about getting a ticket—*almost*.

That's *really* winning!

Again, this technique won't work every time, but it will some, if not most of the time. You're *definitely* better off than if you don't use it.

### Feel, felt, found
One of the most well-known sales techniques is the "Feel, felt, found" technique.

When a prospect has an objection based on a preconceived idea, and you know they're wrong but telling them will only kill the sale, you make your case in a different way. That's where feel, felt, and found come into play.

It might go something like this:

"Ms. Prospect, I understand how you *feel*. Many people in your situation have *felt* the exact same way. However, in researching this further, they *found* that the . . ." and then you finish the sentence with what's appropriate.

It's especially powerful when you include yourself in the discovery.

"I understand how you *feel*. In fact, *I felt* . . ." (stressing "I" instead of "many people" as you did above) ". . . *I felt* the exact same way. What I *found* is . . ." and then complete your thought in the positive.

The feel, felt, found technique also works well when *Winning Without Intimidation*.

The person you are speaking with says, "That's not our policy and I don't like going against policy!" You might respond by saying, "I understand exactly how you feel. I used to feel the same way about our policy. What I found was that when I use policy as a guide—as a *should* as opposed to a *must*—our customers are happier and the business becomes much more profitable."

You may not have changed that person's mind yet, but you are now in a position to help her without her feeling as though she's being manipulated or coerced.

### Lincoln's tactful disgust letter
One of the books I recommend the most at my seminars is *Lincoln on Leadership*, by Donald T. Phillips. This inspiring and very practical book displays President

101

Lincoln's absolute mastery at *Winning Without Intimidation.*

A very tactful and humble man, Lincoln would get his point across in such a way that one could not be offended, even by the president's stern criticism.

The following is a letter Lincoln wrote to General Joseph Hooker, right after Hooker was assigned to his new post. Lincoln actually handed this famous letter to the general immediately after a meeting between the two of them.

Major General Hooker:

General.

I have placed you at the head of the Army of the Potomac. Of course, I have done this upon what appears to me to be sufficient reasons. And yet I think it best for you to know that there are some things in regard to which, I am not quite satisfied with you. I believe you to be a brave and skillful soldier, which, of course, I like. I also believe you do not mix politics with your profession, in which you are right. You have confidence in yourself, which is valuable, if not an indispensable quality. You are ambitious, which, within reasonable bounds, does good rather than harm. But I think that during Gen. Burnside's command of the Army, you have taken counsel of your ambition, and thwarted him as much as you could, in which you did a great wrong to the country, and to a most meritorious and honorable brother officer. I have heard, in such a way as to believe it, of your recently saying that both the Army and the Government needed a Dictator. Of course it was not for this, but in spite of it, that I have given you the command. Only those generals who gain successes, can set up dictators. What I now ask of you is military success, and I will risk the dictatorship. The government will support you to the utmost of its ability, which is neither more nor less than it has done and will do for all commanders. I much fear that the spirit which you have aided to infuse into the Army, of criticizing their Commander, and withholding confidence from him, will now turn upon you. I shall assist you as far as I can, to put it down. Neither you,

102

nor Napoleon, if he were alive again, could get any good out of an army, while such a spirit prevails in it.

And now, beware of rashness. Beware of rashness, but with energy, and sleepless vigilance, go forward, and give us victories.

Yours very truly
A. Lincoln

I could read that letter 100 times and not get tired of it. Lincoln masterfully let Hooker know he was not at all happy about what he did, but first—and throughout the letter—he praised the general's many attributes.

I loved the part where he chided Hooker about expressing his belief in dictatorship. "Only those generals who gain successes can set up dictators." In other words, talk is cheap, Joe. Keep your foolish thoughts to yourself and show everyone you can actually win this thing.

What works in a letter can also work on the telephone or in person. Before criticizing, focus upon the other person's strengths. Build them up before the criticism, and afterwards, too. As Lincoln so expertly did—at all times and during that letter to General Hooker—end by letting the person know you are behind him all the way and have total confidence in his abilities.

We'll talk more about the wise and diplomatic 16th president. As far as I'm concerned, the book *Lincoln on Leadership* is a must read for *Winning Without Intimidation*.

**Focus on your similarities as opposed to your differences**
We are all different, yet we are truly very much the same. When two people are trying to get what they want from each other, they usually see more differences then similarities. But when you can focus on, and bring up, the similarities, you are definitely a step closer to *Winning Without Intimidation*.

Abraham Lincoln had deep personal differences with both his Secretary of War, Edwin Stanton, and his Secretary of State, William Seward. To show you what kind of man Lincoln was, he had hired each of them for their posts knowing the lack of appreciation and outright disrespect they both had for him. Seward even blatantly tried to undermine the president and his decisions on a number of occasions. Neither of them believed that Lincoln was qualified and competent to lead the country through crisis. But each was the best qualified man for the job.

Lincoln looked for the good in both of them, the *similarities* he had with them. He found there were many, including love for, and a deep commitment to, their country. He began spending more time getting to know each man and having them get to know him. He was able to turn them into two of his closest and most loyal allies. That's a leader!

Remember the saying, "A mighty person is one who can control their emotions and make of an enemy a friend?" One of the many quotes attributed to Mr. Lincoln that I've always enjoyed is, "I don't like that man very much . . . I'm going to have to get to know him better."

When you enter into a transaction with someone where you're attempting to Win Without Intimidation, stretch your mind and imagination in order to focus on similarities and—very importantly—make the other person aware of them as well. This goes back to establishing rapport, and it will also show you both where you actually have the same or similar goals and outcomes in mind. Once you can focus on those mutual goals, the individual challenges will begin to work themselves out naturally and automatically.

**Third-party explanations for changing another person's way of thinking**

Since no one likes to be corrected, direct criticism—unless a person's self esteem level hovers around the level of "excellent"—will usually deal a blow to his ego. That will make him more resistant to change. How do you correct someone in such a manner that he doesn't end up feeling defensive and he gets to save face as well?

The "third-party explanation" is usually very effective.

Simply tell a story using yourself in the role of the other person, with you being corrected by a knowledgeable third-party.

Let's pretend your assistant has been slow in updating himself on the newest methods for using the company computer, and it's costing you time and money. You could insist he either come in and learn what he needs to know in his spare time, or lose his job. Will that increase his loyalty to you and improve his job performance? Probably not.

You're the boss, you could fire him. I forgot to mention, however, that in every other way he is excellent, and—if such an employee actually ever exists—he's indispensable to you. He knows you and what you like. He's personable with your clients and they like and feel comfortable with him. The best thing is to persuade him to do whatever it takes to master the newest methods for learning the computer. Let's try the third-party explanation.

"Roger, when I first started with this company, I had a real challenge. Some of the new methods being implemented really intimidated me. My boss, Mary James—who I had a lot of respect for and who I know really appreciated my work—told me, 'You know, Bob, your value to the company will really increase if you can master this new material. After all, there're a lot of people coming right out of college who already know these things, and the best way to keep and increase your value within the company is to do whatever you have to do to keep up-to-date."

What happened there?

The point is made, yet you never ordered Roger to do what was necessary. You simply related, with yourself as the target, what would probably happen regarding his value to the company, depending upon the action he chose to take.

When someone you love is not doing what's needed to improve their rate of success in accomplishing their life's goals, you could say, "Hey, you need to read more books and hang around better quality people." Or you might try something more effective, the third-party explanation. "You know, a very wealthy man named Steve Whitman once told me the only difference between where you are now in your life and where you'll be five years from now is the people you associate with and the books you read."

A man I admire very much once told me, "The third-party explanation will go a lot further in *Winning Without Intimidation* than simply telling a person what to do."

Hey, wasn't *that* a third-party explanation?

### Accept the blame and give the credit

You may be a leader or manager looking to accomplish team success on a long-term project. It will almost always be to your advantage to be known as a leader who is quick to take the blame for failures and quick to give away the credit for successes.

We all know of managers or supervisors whose teams slave away, yet they take the credit.

Does that inspire the troops to work overtime on future projects?

Does that encourage their loyalty?

No, it does not.

What if the team members get to feel the pride of being credited? How about knowing they can stretch themselves and even make mistakes without being publicly "called on the carpet," because they're *safe* with you in the lead?

It's difficult to make great advancements without a few failures from which to learn, isn't it? To know the leader is with and for them all the way gives people the opportunity to grow, work harder, and produce more beneficial results for the team. If the leader takes the blame publicly, and gives them the credit publicly, their motivation and incentive is raised one-hundred fold.

I love what President Ronald Reagan said: "It's amazing what you can accomplish in this town [Washington, D.C.], if you don't care who gets the credit." As the leader, which do you want more, the victory or the credit? If you're the team leader for enough victories, you'll eventually get the big credit.

This was another area in which Abraham Lincoln excelled. According to Donald T. Phillips in *Lincoln on Leadership*, during the president's last public address before his assassination, he exclaimed to the crowd, "No part of the honor, for plan or execution, is mine. To General Grant, his skillful officers, and brave men, all belongs."

Everyone knows how hard and skillfully Lincoln worked during the war. People will know about your efforts as well. The less you congratulate yourself, the more your reputation will continue to *do it for you* in the eyes of both your team and the public.

### Being snubbed or disrespected

When someone you'll be seeing again snubs you or acts disrespectful, you may feel it's something you just cannot or should not ignore. Still, a personal confrontation may not achieve the desired results. Don't call her on it then and there. Keep your posture positive and from then on stay polite and simply show subtle signs of your displeasure.

Let's take the case of a waitress at a brand new restaurant I'd been patronizing since they opened. I had always treated her with respect as I try to do with everyone, and had always left generous tips. But her service and attitude began to change in a negative way, which affected my dining experience. From then on, I showed the same level of respect and politeness, but was just a little bit less outgoing and responsive, and tipped her significantly less. She came around really quickly.

I don't believe it was just the tip, although I'm certain that got her attention. People sense when you're not quite behaving the same to them—especially when you are usually friendly and complimentary. If you remain polite, but forgo the other qualities you usually display, they'll understand something is wrong, and they'll usually correct it all by themselves.

If they come right out and ask, "Is anything wrong?" then you have the opportunity—in a very polite way—to explain your side. It's great if you can use the "I message" we talked about earlier.

You may be asking, "If somebody does something that bothers you, why not let them know right then and there, instead of playing games?"

The answer is, depending upon the situation, that may not be the most effective way to handle the situation. There are times when it is, and if that's the case, take care of it right away by being direct. When doing so either won't get the point across correctly, or you don't feel the person will be able to handle it without being defensive, then use the technique just discussed. It will work much more often than not.

### *Winning Without Intimidation* by playing one source off the other

Remember when, as a kid, you'd play one parent off the other when negotiating for a certain result? You'd say, "Can I go over to Joey's?" Your mom said to ask Dad.

Instead of asking your father, "Can I go over to Joey's?" if you were really resourceful, you'd say, "I told Mom I'm going to Joey's, she just wants me to get your okay first."

Positions things a little bit differently, doesn't it?

You can use that approach as a grownup as well.

When I was a television news anchor, I was known for having a knack for being able to get on-air comments from newsmakers who usually didn't want to comment at all. And I was certainly *not* a journalist . . . I was simply a good *reader* of news. There's a big difference.

On the other hand, the reporter I was teamed with, named Erin, was an excellent journalist with a deep understanding of the issues and an ability to put together a story which could truly educate and involve people. The running joke between us was Erin could never understand how someone with such an amazing lack of understanding of journalism could get practically anyone to talk to him. I simply used the technique of playing one source off the other.

Here's an example: Mayor Hyman would generally be on one side of an issue and Commissioner Balbontin on the other. Each would refuse to be interviewed by the media. I would get on the phone and first call Mayor Hyman. With a sound of indignation in my voice I would say, "Mr. Mayor, this issue is being heard by a lot of people and I will absolutely *not* give the commissioner air time without you having a chance to state your position on the matter. Absolutely not!" He would thank me and agree to go on the air.

I could then tell the commissioner that the mayor had the opportunity to air his views and I would ". . . absolutely *not* allow that without giving you, Mr. Commissioner, the opportunity to do the same. It's only fair."

You can do the same thing in practically any area of *Winning Without Intimidation.*

"Ms. Sales Prospect, we are rolling out our product in your area beginning next month, and I absolutely refuse to present it to your competition without at least giving you the opportunity to learn about it as well."

Be sure and choose the right situation to use this technique. It won't work unless the setting is right, with two or more people who can be equally affected. In the right circumstances it works like a charm.

### Winning *with* Intimidation (only as a last resort, of course)

Every so often a situation arises where the only way you can get what you want is by intimidating the right person at the right time. This is not something I love doing, but if there's no other choice and time is of the essence, you do what you have to do.

I was heading out to the local airport to get a quick comment on camera with then Governor Bob Graham. Surprisingly enough, we were the only reporters there, but I guess the others figured they'd do their interviews at the big meeting he'd be addressing later that evening. With camera in hand, the two of us went to greet his private plane.

Unfortunately, we couldn't find out where it was landing. Obviously this information was not for public or media knowledge. We saw a car at an intersection, and we asked the people if they knew where the governor's plane would be landing. They assured us they had no idea, but something told me they weren't being 100 percent truthful.

We kept our eye on their car and trailed them to the landing sight. As we pulled up, the head guy—the one who assured us they had no idea what was happening—admitted that, "Yes, this is the governor's plane, but he wasn't planning on any interviews until tonight."

Like most of you, I hate being lied to, so there was no way I wasn't going to get this interview right now.

Still attempting to "win without intimidation," I said, "Well, we'd appreciate a short sound bite if you'd be so kind as to arrange it." He patronizingly replied that he'd just said that wasn't in the plans, but we were welcome to

110

get one tonight. Knowing that he wasn't going to be interested in the fact that now I wanted an exclusive, especially since I had hustled out to the airport when none of the others had, I didn't bother telling him that. I said, "Well, let's give the governor an opportunity to tell his constituents how happy he is to be in this fine city, and then I'll ask him one quick question about his speech tonight." His response, with a touch of superiority in his voice was, "Well, that will be up to the governor—won't it?"

It was now time to win *with* intimidation, because that was the only option I could see working. I looked toward my camera person and said, "Ellen, roll the camera starting right now. We'll get a nice shot of the plane landing, and the governor coming out and walking right past us into his car, refusing to address the citizens of this area. And we'll have the camera and microphone right there, so that the viewers can form their own opinions of his silence."

That was a ludicrous, meaningless threat if there ever was one. I also knew it would be easier for them to get him in front of the camera for a few words than explain to him later why they allowed a jerky reporter like myself to cause any kind of trouble. There was no reason for him not to do a quick interview. His aide was just displaying his power. (Ego—remember?) He met his boss at the plane and obviously told him the right thing, because the governor walked towards us, all smiles. He was quite gracious.

It was an easy interview, we got our story, he looked good and we all lived happily ever after.

Sometimes, slight intimidation is necessary, however, use that only as a last resort. I'd rather have won over that aide with kindness and then have been in a position to have him on my side later on if needed. Fortunately, it never was—needed I mean. But how can you ever know for sure until there are no more tomorrows?

111

### Making the best out of an uncomfortable situation

After our interview, the governor chatted with us and asked for our cards—mine and Ellen's. I'm not sure why, possibly to give us a feeling of importance. After all, it was people like us—the press—he really wanted on his side. No wonder he's a successful politician. He's now a United States Senator and there's talk he might run again for Governor of Florida.

He made the best out of an uncomfortable situation for both himself and his aide. For all the governor knew or was told about the situation, I was a reporter out to get him. I wasn't, but that's probably what his aide told him. The governor was out to do the right thing. Turn a potential enemy into a friend. That's *Winning Without Intimidation*.

### Be consistent in your actions

Consistency in our actions is one of the best techniques for *Winning Without Intimidation*. It should become an important part of our lives. We all know people who run hot and cold. They are *this* way one day and *that* way the next.

Maybe I'm simply describing their personality. One minute he is the nicest person in the world, the next, a virtual monster. She says one thing one minute, and the next moment seems to have totally changed her mind. These types are—at best—annoying, and—at worst—nearly impossible to relate to and work for or with. You never know where you stand with these people.

On the other hand, what about the rocks? Those consistently consistent people who have been, are, and will always be *exactly the same*. Seems they never change. There is a comfort with those people—isn't there?

Negotiating authority Roger Dawson suggests that's exactly what made Ronald Reagan so popular and successful as a politician. He was consistent. You could count on him. People knew where he would stand on any issue that came up. Regardless of whether they agreed with his view or not, people felt secure in their knowledge of him as a leader. What he stood for yesterday was what he stood for today and what he would stand for tomorrow.

I was watching a news report showing speeches the president made when he was running for governor of California some 20 years earlier. His words were nearly exactly the same then as they were during his campaign for the presidency. People laughed at that, as though he were "found out."

But that's exactly what made him so successful! People of any political belief always knew where Mr. Reagan stood. It's the same as the young child who can have only one piece of chocolate for dessert or can watch only 30 minutes of television per evening. He might not agree with your decision, but he feels very secure in the fact that he knows his limits with you. He's secure with your sense of consistency in decision making.

**When in a dispute or negotiation, present the other person's side first**

When negotiating or trying to win in a disagreement, always present the other person's case first.

This is a tactic Abraham Lincoln applied quite often as an attorney. As mentioned earlier, Lincoln would highlight points *of the other side's case*. If a person didn't know better, they would think he was representing the opposition! That's how far he took this idea. He covered facts he knew would be brought up by the opposition anyway, but in bringing them up first, he had an opportunity to show his sense of fair play.

This softened the natural defense mechanism of the judge and jurors who were always prepared to hear a one-sided monologue. When Lincoln did that, in essence he said to judge and jury, "Hey, I'm looking at this case strictly from the point of merit as a fair and open-minded person just seeking the truth—*as you are.*"

He firmly established his honesty, integrity, and sense of fair play and justice. A pretty winning place to start for an attorney—don't you think? Of course, he would then present a much stronger case for his side, which, because of the jury's positive feeling towards him, was even more persuasive and effective.

When you are in a situation with another person where there is a definite difference of opinion, you can apply this technique. Present some of the facts from their side first to essentially say to them, "Hey, there are two sides to our discussion. We're both intelligent, nice people who have points we believe in."

When you're applying for a raise, let the boss know, "I understand where you're coming from. The budget is tough, sales are down, there isn't a lot of discretionary monies."

You've established yourself, your understanding of your boss's situation and your base of honesty. You're in a great position to give him your side of the story. "In the short year I've been with the company, production in my area has been up seven percent and expenses are down five percent, justifying a raise of X dollars a  year."

That's *Winning Without Intimidation*.

### Remain humble after your victory

Whether it's only a game of Monopoly® played with friends or a big sale in which you've won out over your competition, NEVER GLOAT or act cocky. Always be humble. If you aren't, the other *players* will go out of their way to make sure you don't win next time, even if *they* have to lose just to keep you from winning. That's simply human nature.

### *Winning Without Intimidation* via the Platinum Rule

Jim Cathcart speaks on the topic of "Relationship

Selling." He has a great book out by that same title. In it, Jim talks about the difference between the Golden Rule and what he calls the "Platinum Rule." The Golden Rule is "Do unto others as you'd have them do unto you." Isn't that a wonderful philosophy to have?

According to Jim, the Platinum Rule goes one giant step further: "Do unto others as THEY'D like to be done unto."

Jim explains that distinct personality types and styles have different ways they like to be treated or dealt with in various situations. This, of course, relates not only to professional sales, but in all facets of *Winning Without Intimidation* in your life and work.

Some people want the "bottom line" right away. Others want to know all the little facts and figures. Certain people want to take time to get to know each other and establish a friendship. Others want to be continually assured that they're making the right decision. Some people want to be worked with and negotiated with *like this* and other people want to be worked with and negotiated with *like that*.

If you want to increase your odds of Winning Without Intimidation in any and all situations—learn how other people like to be dealt with, and deal with them in that way.

### Request instead of order

If you really want to distinguish yourself from the masses, try making requests instead of issuing orders. A person who is used to being *ordered* to perform, such as a waitperson, staff member, hotel employee, etc., will go absolutely out of his way to serve you if you *request* his actions.

Instead of saying to the waiter, "Bring us some more water," or "We need water," say, "When you get a chance, would you please bring us some more water?" Some people might think this would only delay getting the water.

115

Actually the opposite is true. Because you've made that person feel respected, you'll be the *first* person he'll want to make happy.

Instead of an order, make it a request. Instead of, "Joe, make seven copies of these," how about, "Joe, would you run seven copies of these for me, please?" Phrase your "order" in the form of a request and you'll be *Winning Without Intimidation* both in the short- and long-term.

### Be a "Yes Person"

I don't mean the stereotypical "Yes Man" who is always sucking up to the boss. Be a person who—when approached by someone with a new idea—looks for the good in it, rather than what's wrong. Of course, I'm not advising you to say something you don't believe, or lie, or to take action on every idea that comes up. Not at all. I'm saying simply to be encouraging, whether it's a request from a vendor or a friend looking for encouragement regarding a new idea.

I think former Secretary General of the United Nations Dag Hammerskjöld captured the essence of what I mean by being a "Yes Person" in this remark:

"To all that has been—*thanks*.
To all that will be—*yes!*"

Most people look at the negative. When approached with an idea, they respond with, "That'll never work." How about a request from a vendor to look at a new product or service? They typically say things like, "It's not our policy ... It's never been done before ..." Or, "I don't think we can do that."

While the techniques we're reviewing in this series are designed to show how to overcome such attitudes in others, we also need to be aware of them in ourselves. Even if you feel nothing can be done, be supportive. Instead of immediately discouraging the other person, give whatever positive response you can.

You may not agree with a vendor's idea and you may not see the possibilities your friend envisions, but you're certainly rooting for them all the way. Let them know. Offer whatever best wishes and emotional support you can give. This will always result in *Winning Without Intimidation*.

### The letter that's never sent

Have you ever been very angry—furious, flaming, enraged—at someone who mistreated you? Write a scathing, insulting letter. Let it all hang out. Don't hold back. Put it in an envelope and address that envelope and even put a stamp on it if you like. Then, before mailing that letter, tear it up into a thousand pieces!

Your anger will have subsided dramatically, and no one will ever know.

Author and speaker Zig Ziglar gave that wise piece of advice to a woman who approached him after a program to tell him of a personal situation she had gone through, which really roused her resentment. I was standing right there and had occasion to see Zig at his best, taking time to counsel this person right after performing one of his high-energy seminars.

Sometimes it is correct to send a letter expressing resentment of a situation—after waiting a few days before writing it and expressing your feelings diplomatically, of course. But in this case, Zig gave the perfect piece of advice.

That was another one of Abe Lincoln's techniques, too. Sometimes he needed to express his angry feelings just to get it off his chest, so he'd write a letter with every scathing remark and insult he could think of, and then tear it up or file it away forever.

You see, if no one would benefit from that letter being sent and people would be unnecessarily hurt, the letter wouldn't add positively to the situation. The best thing you can do is never send it. But do write it! Writing that letter is wonderful therapy. You'll get your negative feelings off your chest and be very glad you did. Who wants to carry anger like that around?

This is just one more form of *Winning Without Intimidation*.

### Edify, edify, edify

Remember that to *edify* means to build? When you edify a person to someone else, you build them up in that other person's mind. When you edify him to himself, however, you build him in his own mind. The more you do that, the better he'll feel about himself and the better he'll feel about you, too. This leads to long-term *Winning Without Intimidation*.

Edifying someone to a third party plays on the old saying, "If you can't say something nice, don't say anything at all." You can *always* say something nice about someone, and you can always *find* a reason to do so.

Even the most miserable people out there have something about them that we can discover and edify to someone else. This accomplishes two things: Number one, it will probably get back to that person you are edifying, which can only have positive results. Number two, you'll establish yourself in the mind of the person you're speaking to as someone who only has nice things to say about other people.

People enjoy people like that—much more than those who speak negatively of others. Even if *they* are the kind who speaks negatively about people, they'll respect you for your edification of others.

My dad is a tremendous example of a man who only speaks positively and with edification of others. From his wife—my mom—to his kids, friends and even people who, to most others, warrant only unkind words, my dad will always find (sometimes it's a search and a stretch) something nice to say.

118

Husbands and wives often talk about how the love and respect has gone out of their marriage. I notice how, quite often, they are not edifying each other to themselves nor to other people. Both my folks are always edifying or bragging on each other. I have to relate an incident to you that is the essence of edification, while displaying incredible tact and diplomacy.

When I was about 10 or 11 years old, we were having a brand new carpet installed in our home. During the day, we all stayed in one room while the crew boss and his two assistants were laying down the carpet in the rest of the house. The boss was a decent person, but one of those stereotypical "rough around the edges," beer-guzzlin,' hard-livin' guys, who would probably belong to Ralph Kramden's Raccoon Lodge from the old Honeymooner's TV show—if you know what I mean.

At lunchtime, my folks bought pizza for us and the crew. Dad went upstairs to give pizza to the carpet layers and talk with the crew boss about how things were coming along. Since Dad is a great guy and can relate to practically anybody, the boss naturally wanted to ingratiate himself and begin the male bonding process. While this was going on, I was around the corner listening to the conversation.

The boss began by saying, "This is an expensive job. Boy-oh-boy, those women will really spend your money for you, won't they?"

Dad responded by saying, "Well, I'll tell you, when they were right there with you before you had the money, it's a pleasure to do anything for them you possibly can."

That's not exactly the answer this guy expected. He was looking for this to be a conversation between two guys who could talk negatively about their wives which, to him, was the natural thing for men to do. So, he tried again:

"But, gee, they'll really play off that and want to spend all they can, won't they?"

Dad replied as I knew he would: "Hey, when they're

the reason for your success, you really want to know you're doing things they enjoy. There's no greater pleasure."

Strike two. The crew boss tried one more time. "And they'll take that as far as they can, huh?"

Dad responded: "It's just so gratifying to know you've got a wife who's your best friend, and you'd do anything within your power to make her happy."

At this point, I was working hard to keep from laughing, because I knew the guy wanted my dad to at least give in a little bit and say, "Yeah, yeah, I guess that's true." But I knew that wouldn't happen in a million years.

Finally, the boss gave up. Maybe he learned something in that transaction about respecting your spouse. Maybe not. It taught a young boy a lot, though—about the power of respect and edification.

My mom and dad would do anything for each other. After learning about that conversation, would you have any doubt?

You can use this principle not only to Win Without Intimidation in your married life, but in dealing with people in general. If people know you are edifying them, that will lead to long-term *Winning Without Intimidation*. Those people will *want* to give you what you want.

### Winning through delayed gratification

Someone wrongs you. It happens, doesn't it? It certainly does to me. Respond or react? Get even now or wait to win?

Before taking any negative action—or reacting in a negative way toward a person or their actions—pause and ask yourself, "Will my negative reaction strengthen or hurt my relationship or position with this person?"

It might feel good in the short-term to verbally strike back, but will it hurt you in the long run? Probably.

You always have a choice between instant gratification and delayed gratification. Those who consistently "win without intimidation" opt for delayed gratification more often than not.

### There's no winning an argument

It was in Dale Carnegie's book, *How to Win Friends and Influence People*, that I first learned the principle that there really is no way to win an argument. As Mr. Carnegie said, "A man convinced against his will is of the same opinion still." Not to mention the bad will that will probably result with that person. Not effective for *Winning Without Intimidation*.

Abe Lincoln agreed. In *Lincoln on Leadership*, Donald T. Phillips tells how the President reprimanded Capt. James M. Cutts for continually arguing with and verbally abusing another officer. Lincoln pointed out that no person resolved to make the most of himself can spare time for personal conflict. The most famous part of his reprimand was the following:

"Better to give your path to a dog, than be bitten by him in contesting for the right. Even killing the dog would not cure the bite."

In *Winning Without Intimidation*, I recommend you do your best never to argue.

We've been reviewing ideas throughout this book on how to effectively persuade people and get what you want, but every so often you and I will fall victim to "the argument." The lessons on the uselessness of arguing taught by Dale Carnegie and President Lincoln will serve perhaps better than any other single skill in your quest toward *Winning Without Intimidation*.

### Lose the battle, win the war

Sometimes it's okay to lose a small battle in order to win the war. When negotiating, or attempting to win your point without intimidation, don't be afraid to make some minor concessions here and there to get what you're *really* after. You've got to be able to see the big picture.

121

I wrote earlier about the fact that people who have only a certain amount of power don't like to have that power undermined. Even if you convince them you're right, their ego may keep you from persuading them to change. Let them save face by winning a couple of unimportant points that really don't matter much to you. This will allow them to feel as though they didn't get beaten into the ground—gives them a win.

You may even have to invent those small points for them to win. When you do, you must make the other person feel that point was *their* brainchild, their victory. With a little imagination it's easy to do, and the dividends will be well worth it.

### Complaints with humility get better responses

When writing a letter of complaint or leaving a complaint on an answering machine or voice mail, state the facts with humility. If possible, begin your communication with praise. Mention that you certainly don't know nearly as much about that person's position or business as do they. Then, when you mention something that is "right on the mark"—even if it's not positive—your credibility with that person increases even more.

After visiting several different stores of a particular franchise operation and receiving absolutely terrible service at each and every one, I decided to call the company headquarters and voice my displeasure to the CEO himself. He wasn't in, but I did reach his voice mail and decided to simply leave a message.

Since this event took place several years ago, and I didn't realize then there might be a need to remember my words verbatim for use in a book, I can only give you a paraphrasing of my message. I know I can get close to the original words, though, because I would use this same method any time I was in a similar situation. The message went something like this:

"Hi Mr. Smith, this is Bob Burg calling from Jupiter,

122

Florida. If you'd *like* to call me after hearing this message you're welcome to, but it certainly isn't necessary. I'm a fellow entrepreneur and a very loyal and usually quite satisfied customer who has enjoyed using and referring your products for years. I thought you might be interested in a few incidents at your Florida stores.

"Unfortunately—and very unlike my usual experience with your company's excellent customer service people—I was put in a very challenging situation which didn't work to the advantage of your store, myself, or the other customers. Had this event happened once, even twice, I'd have shrugged it off, knowing your company's dedication to your customers. After three separate occurrences—although I don't pretend to know your business—quite frankly, I thought you might want to know.

"If you'd like to speak with me further, my name is Bob Burg and I'm at 561-575-2114. Thank you for your time. Make it a great day."

Do you think I received a response from this huge corporation?

Absolutely. Not from the CEO himself, but from his personal, right-hand man. We spoke on the phone, and not only was he very apologetic, he was very grateful that I called and made him aware of the situation.

People in that position place a lot more importance on a complaint made by someone who acts humbly, logically and civilly. Troubleshooters have to deal with ranters, ravers and screamers all day long. They are a dime a dozen—more like a penny. By positioning yourself politely apart from the negative crowd, you increase your chances dramatically of Winning Without Intimidation.

**Treat everyone the exact same way—with R-E-S-P-E-C-T**

Treat every person—in every job, position or station in life—the same way, and with the same respect as you would, say, a millionaire CEO of a Fortune 500 company.

123

Not only is it the right thing to do, but you never know when you're going to need that person for something important. That's why it's so necessary to develop the habit of *Winning Without Intimidation.*

It happens by way of habit: When the action is so *ingrained* you do it without thinking. Do you show respect to the man or woman at the toll-gate? How about the waitperson? The person at the cash register? The custodian?

Making this show of respect a habit leads to both short- and long-term *Winning Without Intimidation.*

### A good test

When you feel good about yourself—knowing you're acting out of fairness and justice—it shows up in your general demeanor and goes a long way towards both short and long-term *Winning Without Intimidation.*

As a personal test, to make sure you're staying on the right track, ask yourself, "Is what I'm doing serving the other person—as well as myself?"

### Match and mirror

Earlier in the book, we looked at Neuro Linguistic Programming or NLP—a technology which is very effective in helping to establish rapport with another person. Another phase of using NLP is matching a person in as many ways as possible without, of course, being too obvious about it.

For instance, as the person you're with begins to rest her hand on her chin—or cross her legs, or fold her arms—wait for a moment, and then slowly do the same. That's called mirroring, and it helps establish rapport.

You don't want to be obvious about it and "get caught," so to speak. That will "break" rapport, not build it. It takes practice to notice and mirror others effectively.

Matching and mirroring are totally natural processes when two people are already in rapport. You're simply helping the process, so the other person feels comfortable with you sooner rather than later. Even matching another person's breathing can do wonders. With a little practice it's a snap.

According to NLP authority Susan Stageman of Dallas, Texas, when done correctly, matching breathing brings two people totally "in sync." The person whose breathing you are matching will never even know why. Can you see how this would help greatly in *Winning Without Intimidation*?

Since learning about the technology of Neuro Linguistic Programming from Susan and various books, I've found it to be a real bonus in my life.

Another great technique is to match the volume of the person's voice. If she's talking softly, just do the same thing. Also, increase your tempo to her speed, or speak a little more slowly if that's what she is doing.

In establishing rapport over the telephone, voice matching can be very effective.

### Obvious ... but utilized?

Treat a person nicely and they'll go out of their way for you a lot quicker and a lot more strongly than if you yell at them and insult them.

Isn't that obvious? Then why do we see so many people yelling, insulting and threatening people?

Please, think about that the next time you are about to "react" to someone's actions or inactions. How much better could you make your chances of *Winning Without Intimidation* by simply "responding" with kindness, compassion, and respect?

### Make sure your compliments are noticed

Tell the manager that the waitperson was fantastic. Tell the waitperson that the food was wonderful and to please pass that compliment on to the chef.

You want to make sure your compliments about someone get heard by that person. We also want them to know from whom it originated.

Why?

Not only will they feel good about it, a reward from you for their service, but they'll feel good about you and be even more anxious to please the next time you come in. This isn't only for restaurant service. It works in virtually any area in which you desire to Win Without Intimidation.

Does this really work? Absolutely!

I've had chefs come out of the kitchen and walk over to my table to personally thank me for my kind words.

### A restaurant tip that gets results

When sending food back to be re-cooked, or cooked differently, or because of any other challenge, address the waitperson beginning with these words: "Please, tell the chef the dinner is absolutely excellent. There's just one thing, if I could have . . ." and finish the request with what you want.

Remember to make sure the waitperson intends to share the praise. Watch how nicely your meal comes out this time.

### Just a thought

Each and every year, millions of 1/4 inch drill bits are sold, and yet nobody buying any one of these actually wants a 1/4 inch drill bit . . .

Why do they buy them? Because they want a 1/4 inch *hole*.

What's my point, and what does that have to do with *Winning Without Intimidation*? People do things for reasons that aren't always obvious, and we need to know what those reasons are.

Not everyone has the same reasons for buying a given product. Some base their decision on price, others on quality and still others on style.

Not everyone reacts or responds to a situation for the

same reasons we might. When *Winning Without Intimidation*, you have to find out what will motivate that person to buy your 1/4 inch drill, or what will motivate him to do whatever it is you want him to do.

### A quick telephone technique

For sure-fire, long-term *Winning Without Intimidation* —especially if the relationship you are establishing is being done on the telephone—here's a simple little technique which will always work for you. It will never come back to haunt you, either. I learned this from telephone sales authority David Allan Yoho.

Hang up last!

Isn't it a lousy feeling when just a nanosecond after saying good-bye to someone, you hear the loud, impersonal "click" of the telephone being plunked down on it's holder?

Well, *you* might not find it annoying, but many people do. More than just annoying, it gives people the feeling that, "Hey, that person really wanted to get off the phone with me. Why? Am I just another sale or number to them?"

Give the other person time to hang up the telephone first. If you feel that person—for whatever reason—is waiting for you to hang up first, just wait a few seconds, and then lightly place the phone on its receiver.

This must be practiced to become a habit. I let new office staff know that this is very important to me, and I've had to remind them to make it a habit. If I was walking past someone's desk and heard him hang up quickly after saying good-bye, I questioned him about it. If he told me it was "just a friend" on the phone, or someone he knew real well, I told him that didn't matter. What we do as a bad habit, we will tend to do all of the time. We have to completely replace that bad habit with a more positive habit.

**Good morning!**
Always smile and greet people cheerfully.

People are never exactly sure how your attitude will be when you're approaching them. Most people deal with many unhappy, even mean and nasty people. That's what they've learned to expect. When you smile and say, "Good morning," you've set the tone for everybody to win.

But please, don't ever say, "How ya doing?" Actually, most people don't even pronounce the "g" at the end of "doing." It's more like, "how ya doin'?" When a person says, "How ya doin'?" doesn't it sound as though they are actually saying, "I don't really care *how ya doin'*?"

Nothing bugs me more than to have somebody greet me with "How ya doin'?" and then walk right past me without even waiting for my answer. I can't imagine many things more rude. Okay, I can, but you get my point.

Be sincere in your greeting.

Recently I crossed paths with a person, and as our eyes met, it was obvious he wasn't very happy. One option would have been to just ignore him completely, but would I really have been making any contribution to the world that way? I flashed a big grin and said, "Good morning!" You should have seen his face brighten as he greeted me in return!

Maybe he'll greet someone the same way a bit later on, and that person will do the same to someone else. If you figure those people will all have a much healthier attitude as they encounter other people during the day, think how many lives were potentially affected positively with that one brief greeting. It made both of us feel better about ourselves at the same time. There wasn't any cost, but there sure was a reward.

Actually, two rewards: One was the good feeling we both got from giving the greeting, and the other was the practice at *internalizing* greeting someone the right way. This will come in handy in the future, I guarantee it.

**Another way of asking**

One way to get someone on your side really quickly is to "apologize."

Sound strange?

"*I'm sorry* to bother you, could you please . . . ," and then complete your request. Asking in that way will, more often than not, elicit a quick and helpful response. This is true whether you're asking someone on the street for directions or the government employee a question about the form you need to fill out.

You're making the person feel needed and acknowledging to him that you know he is important enough to have his time constraints considered. You're being humble and courteous.

This simple technique has helped me Win Without Intimidation throughout the years.

**Beginning a telephone sale**

When calling someone on the telephone, here's a good way to begin the conversation and clear the moment. You may need their time to listen to your sales presentation, or maybe you need a special exemption from your kid's principal. Doesn't matter—it still works.

Simply say something like, "Ms. Conrad, this is Bob Burg, do you have a quick minute or did I call at a really awful time?"

There are people from the "old school of sales" who'll say, "Burg, why would you give this person an opportunity to get rid of you?" That's not really what I'm doing.

If she answers, "Actually, yes, I'm in the middle of a conference and I'm surrounded by four clients with a deadline for completion on another project in 30 minutes," then you can pretty much safely assume you wouldn't have her full attention anyway. In fact, you would only cause her to resent you, which would make *Winning Without Intimidation* a whole lot more difficult.

What a person will usually say is either, "Well, I've got

a few minutes, how may I help you?" Or he might even say, "No, this is fine." By showing him you respect his time, you are honoring him and making him feel good about himself. And of course, that will more quickly establish rapport, which leads to *Winning Without Intimidation*.

### Confessing ignorance
Can you and I put our egos aside in order to get what we want? If not, let's work on it. It's a key to *Winning Without Intimidation*.

You can always easily confess your ignorance in the area that the person with whom you're dealing is skilled. Only if it's true of course, but usually you're willing to pay someone a fee to perform a particular job or service because they specialize in that particular area.

In my case, it's easy to admit ignorance in many areas and be totally truthful about it. As I've said, it's easy for me to tell the mechanic, "Man, I am the most ignorant person in the world when it comes to cars."

I know what some of you are thinking: Burg, did you just set yourself up to be taken advantage of? No, I don't think so. I have just used the technique of putting my fate in this person's hands in a way that makes her feel important. It makes her feel good about herself.

I've paved the way for her to take care of me. People are like that. We all like to use our skills for the benefit of others—*when* those others seek our help with politeness and respect.

I've use this tactic in countless situations, and I tend to get treated better and more fairly than most other people—certainly better than those who take the opposite approach.

### A key thought
Please keep this thought in mind continually. In essence, it's what this book is all about and why it's so

130

very possible to consistently find yourself *Winning Without Intimidation*. Here's the thought:

**Make people feel good about themselves!!!!!!!!!**

This is so important, I want to repeat it.

# Make people feel good about themselves!!!!!!!!!

### Admit mistakes

For some reason—probably ego—there are people who have a real challenge doing this one, yet it's really so simple and effective. You know what it is? Apologize. Apologize when you are wrong. Sometimes even if you aren't.

"Umh! I apologize. I was wrong."

Look at your own life and work. Isn't the level of respect you have for people who will admit their mistakes and apologize much higher than for the people who won't admit their mistakes?

We humans seem to have a challenge with this—with friends, family, co-workers, and practically everyone else. If we can get past that and simply admit when we're wrong, we'll have one more effective power-tool we can plug in and use for constantly *Winning Without Intimidation*.

In his powerful book, *Dynamic People Skills*, Dexter Yager says, "One thing I do when potential conflicts arise with people is to apologize. Most people are afraid to apologize for anything at all. That's because they don't understand the power of it." He adds, "I'll apologize at the drop of a hat. I'll apologize for things that are my fault and things that are not my fault. I've found out that apologies are magical. They take the pressure off the situation, off the other person and put it on me. That stops conflict immediately."

What I appreciate most about Dexter's message is the fact that when we can do this—apologize when we are wrong and *especially when we aren't*—it shows a tremendous amount of self-confidence and self-esteem. Your gesture will ultimately be appreciated by the other person, and you will have gained a great deal of respect at the same time.

### Focus on the solution, not the problem

Those of us who practice the art of *Winning Without Intimidation* realize that, day after day, we must persuade those who are lazy, stubborn, arrogant, unimaginative, or whatever else, to find ways to do things they ordinarily would not do. How often do you hear someone respond to your request with, "We don't do it that way here," or, "It's not our policy," or, " Sorry, it can't be done." Or one of my least favorites, "I tried it once and it doesn't work."

My good friend, Thomas Hudson, has some excellent advice for that. He calls it "living in the solution, not the problem."

You do that anyway, don't you? Sure you do. Your challenge then, is to get the *other* person to do that: Get that person out of the problem mode and into the solution mode. You need to tactfully let that person know you are both going into that mode, and together you'll come up with a solution. As long as you do this with an attitude of kindness and helpfulness, it will work. And, as much as you possibly can, let the other person feel as though the solution was theirs.

Becoming solution oriented applies in matters of the heart as well as business. Dexter Yager points out that "when a problem develops in a relationship, your goal is to solve the problem, not win the war." This relates to all aspects of *Winning Without Intimidation*, doesn't it?

Mr. Yager suggests that we need to put ego (the normal human desire to be right) aside and not let that desire control us. He says that if we do let desire take over, we confuse the issue and contaminate the situation until no one can distinguish the true problem, let alone its solution.

According to Dexter, "Most people in a conflict situation haven't taken time to figure out what they want themselves, much less what the other person wants." The way to ensure this doesn't happen is to have the solution in mind.

**If you could prove to yourself that . . .**

The smallest change in phraseology can make a big difference in how your ideas come across to another person.

Has anyone ever said to you—perhaps while simply attempting to prove a point or wanting you to buy something from them—"If I can convince you that (such and such) will save you money . . . ," or, "If I can prove to you that . . . ," didn't you sort of say to yourself, "This guy isn't going to convince me of anything!" I know I have. It's human nature to resist when challenged, and the phrases, "If I can convince you . . . ," or, "If I can prove to you that . . . ," is certainly a challenge.

Here's a more effective way to open someone to your "proof." (This is another gem I first learned from Zig Ziglar.) Instead of saying, "If I can convince you that . . . ," say, "If you could convince *yourself* that . . ." Continue with the benefit you want them to understand, such as ". . . this will save you money in the long run." Or, "If you could prove to yourself that the right way is to so and so . . ."

You've allowed that person to take control and convince himself or prove something to herself. Who is she going to resist—herself and her *own* ideas? No way!

Practice this technique enough so that when the situation arises, the correct way of phrasing your point will come out naturally. After all, if you could convince yourself that this idea would help you to more effectively Win

133

Without Intimidation, wouldn't you want to have it perfected?

**I might be wrong about this ...**
This technique is just another one of those lead-in phrases that makes a person more receptive to your request or challenge. It's very simple and goes like this:

"Mr. Thomas, *I might be wrong about this—it certainly wouldn't be the first time.* I'm wondering though ... " and then fill in the rest with your particular challenge or request.

Do you need to tell a manager about an error on your bill?

"*I might be wrong about this—it certainly wouldn't be the first time.* I'm wondering though, wasn't this charge right here only $17 instead of $117?"

That's much more effective than telling others they are wrong and must fix it. This technique is apt to lead you more easily toward *Winning Without Intimidation.*

**Win Without Intimidation just by listening**
There are times when absolutely the best thing we can do in order to prove our point is to listen—really listen—to the *other* person. Just listen until they are finished. Let them talk themselves out and know they've been heard. This works in all types of situations.

When I was in television advertising sales, I walked into a business on a cold-call in an attempt to meet the owner and help him purchase advertising time on my station. As soon as he discovered my line of work, he began a verbal assault on my profession. He ranted about why he would never "in a million years" buy TV advertising time.

Despite the natural human urge to snap back at him or defend my position, I just let him talk—thinking to myself, "well, this sale isn't going to happen." After a while, his tone began to soften. He started talking about a friend who had done well through television advertising, and I began thinking, "I don't believe this . . . this guy's gonna buy after all." And he did. Without my saying one word!

Does it always work out like that? No, but letting people talk themselves out is a good beginning, and you never know!

After the person talks himself out and has nothing left to say, it's great to let him know you understand his concerns. Remember the Feel, Felt and Found technique we discussed earlier? Use that, and then ask if there are any additional "*questions*" he might have.

Using the word "questions," instead of "problems," is much more effective. When they say they don't have any, you're in an excellent position to handle the situation in any way you may deem effective.

### You know a lot more about this than I do

One extremely effective phrase is, "*You know a lot more about this than I do*, how would you approach . . . ?" Fill in the blank with your particular challenge. You've paid that person's ego a very high compliment and put him in control. Usually, that person will be only too glad to live up to the high level of expectation you've just set for him.

### Begin a criticism with genuine and sincere praise

Another technique Dale Carnegie addressed in *How To Win Friends And Influence People* was a very effective way of dispensing criticism without eliciting resentment: Begin your criticism with praise. The praise *must* be genuine and sincere, or it will likely fall upon deaf ears. But if a person first hears something nice and positive about herself, she will be less defensive and feel better about the words of correction that will follow. Then, after saying what must be said, finish with another kind word or positive thought.

Here's an example: "Don, one thing I've always admired about you is the hard work and pride that you usually put into your projects. That's why I was a bit surprised that the project you just completed was far below your usual standards. It's happened to all of us at one time or another, and I know you well enough to know that's not going to happen again."

What you've done is complimented Don and criticized not him, but his performance. You let him know it's happened to you, too, so he's not alone and doesn't feel singled-out. You then complimented him again while giving an underlying hint that better things are definitely expected. Regardless of the situation or circumstances in which you use this technique, it will motivate the other person to perform correctly. It will absolutely help you Win Without Intimidation.

**Quick tip—Seven words that will come back to haunt you**

There are seven words that will eventually come back to haunt you sooner or later—especially if said often enough after not treating a person with the proper respect and sense of human dignity. Here are those seven words:

"I'll never need him for anything anyway."

**Help them to be happy to do what they don't want to do**

True *Winning Without Intimidation* is being so skillful as to help a person change their attitude totally about a certain position, task, or situation, from negative to positive. Here's a great example of what I mean:

Years ago, when I first began appearing on a number of the major sales and motivational rally programs throughout the country, I would be the opening speaker for either a major sports figure or a more well-known professional speaker than myself. He or she would be the person whose big name would draw the crowd, and I would give the audience the how-to information on business networking—my main topic.

One person was promoting a series of programs to take place monthly in the same city. Included in the 12-month advertising materials were some of the most famous names in the speaking profession—and there was *me*. Actually, I was thrilled to even to be included in the promotional materials. Talk about a thrill for a young speaker! Thirteen speakers were listed in all. Every speaker would have the stage to himself for the entire evening except two: The speaker I would open for and, of course, myself. Ours would be the very first program in the 12-month series.

When that speaker (an excellent speaker, by the way) saw the schedule, he immediately called the promoter—ego in the lead—to ask *why* he was the only major speaker who had to have an opener. Didn't the promoter think he was good enough to carry the program by himself?

The promoter, thinking quickly, told him it was because he was so well-known and I wasn't, that I needed a big name to establish my credibility—especially for this all-important first program of the series. Our excellent, and formerly ego-deflated speaker, gladly accepted that with a smile and was fine to do his program on, of all things, *How to Improve Your Self-Esteem*.

### Declining an offer graciously

When you're involved in a negotiation and you're offered something you feel is worthless, offer *lavish appreciation* for their *thinking* of you like that. "I'm honored to even be thought of in that way, yet it wouldn't be feasible in this case." Those offering will understand they are way off base as far as any chance of making a deal with you, but you haven't offended them with your response.

So many people offend the other person when turning down an offer—and it just closes doors and makes for a

137

loss. If you employ tact, you let others save face, and they'll come back with a more realistic offer—if it's at all possible.

## Keeping the door open without being at all committal

Recently, I was referred to a rather large company for my program on business networking. In negotiations, the key decision maker and I had a definite challenge coming to terms regarding my fee. After a somewhat lengthy conversation, we came to the mutual agreement that we were just too far apart. His last comment to me was to feel free to call him if I decided I could do their program for the final fee he offered.

Immediately after the conversation, I wrote a Thank You letter, as I always do. In this short, handwritten note, I thanked him for his time but said absolutely nothing of substance in the letter. I basically said "No," while in no way closing the door to further discussion.

This nice but non-committal note left the door open for him to call me if he decided he could pay me the final fee *I* offered. He could feel comfortable in calling me, knowing he wouldn't have to eat humble pie.

Did he call? Not yet, but this is one of those instances where there's plenty of time for *Winning Without Intimidation*.

## Notice something of *their* interest

If at all possible, notice something which is of interest to, or a source of pride for, the other person. A picture of their child on their desk. Trophies on the wall or something . . . *anything*. But your interest must be genuine, or they'll pick up on your insincerity for sure.

One gentleman in particular was in a position to give me a key referral that would have benefited me greatly in my business. He invited me to his home to discuss the matter with him, letting me know, however, that he was

138

not promising me anything. He was a retired business-man, and the first thing I noticed as we were walking through his garage was a huge display of hand-carved wooden birds. They were fascinating, beautiful and exquisitely made.

"Did you carve those yourself?" I asked.

Guess what we talked about for the next two hours? Did I get the referral? I sure did.

It turned out that in his retirement, he made carvings pretty much day and night. The wooden birds were absolutely incredible. They were also now his primary measurement of self worth and form of satisfaction after a long and distinguished career in business.

Notice what is important or of interest to the other person and you'll be well on your way to *Winning Without Intimidation* effortlessly!

### Another reason to smile

Smile as you are saying something constructive to someone. Particularly when you're telling them some-thing which, if you weren't smiling, could be interpreted as an insult. If you can smile while doing this, it's one of the best ways to build a person while at the same time being constructive.

Picture me smiling as I tell Ken he's not speaking with enough respect to his associate: "See, Ken, when we do that, we usually get the exact opposite response than we want from the other person."

This comes across a lot differently than if I had given him a disgusted look and said the same thing. Practice this. It really works!

My dad is absolutely the *best* in the world at this. Fortunately, I've been able to acquire this skill after much practice.

I am not talking about giving mixed signals (smiling while angry or something similar), but using your smile to simply *soften* a criticism. You know it's working if the person begins to unconsciously mirror your smile—she smiles back at you while she is being criticized.

What a win that is!

### Know your objective and plan your approach

Milo Frank, in his book *How To Make Your Point in 30 Seconds or Less*, talks about knowing your objective and then planning your approach. When, as an objective, you want to get your money back for a defective product or get an exchange on an item you purchased, you need to have an effective, planned approach.

You begin with, "I know good companies like yours stand behind their merchandise."

What has Mr. Frank suggested there?

Basically, that you are giving them something of high value—such as their excellent reputation—to live up to. I really like his quote: "Know what you want, know who can give it to you, and know how to get it." That applies to practically anything you undertake to Win Without Intimidation.

### Doing business for this price is an insurance policy

During a negotiation, another way of warning someone without actually threatening him (remember the implied threat) is what I call the "insurance policy technique." While negotiating the price of a car, I told the car salesperson the following (with tact, of course):

"Mr. Kennedy, if we can't agree on this particular price, I can't *justify* making the purchase right now without investigating further."

"I'm not saying that I won't eventually come back here. I enjoy doing business with you, but I'd have to visit several other dealerships to see if I could get the price I feel I need. In a sense, your coming down xx amount of dollars right now is sort of like" —this is said with a sincere smile— "you buying an insurance policy that I *won't* buy a car from someone else. Of course, I'll understand if you just can't do that."

As I began, I said what I needed to say with a look of kindness, not a scowl. And I told him I couldn't *"justify"* making the purchase now—not that I *won't*. I wanted to help him save face and have him want to help me get what I wanted.

What was the result?

I got my price. And it was a win/win. The dealer still made a profit, and that sale has resulted in several referrals from me to that salesperson. The transaction was handled in a professional way, and that scenario positively set up my next visit. He knows that if I don't get the price I feel I need, I won't be able to *justify* making the purchase now.

### Tidbit regarding compliments

In *How To Have Confidence And Power In Dealing With People*, Les Giblin advises us to form the habit of paying at least three sincere compliments each day. Good idea.

Mr. Giblin talks about syndicated columnist Dr. George Crane suggesting people join what he calls "The Compliment Club." To be a member, all a person has to do is deliberately go out and search for good things in other people that they can compliment.

Why don't you—as training for *Winning Without Intimidation*—make a game out of it and call it "The Compliment Game?" How many days in a row can you go giving out at least, at *least*, five compliments? That's one or more compliments to five different people. Your only competition is yourself, and if you win the game, imagine how much more effective your powers of positive persuasion will become . . .

### Be the host, not the guest

In my book *ENDLESS REFERRALS Network Your Everyday Contacts Into Sales*, I hit upon the technique of positioning yourself as one of the "big people on campus," or "playing the host, not the guest."

When you're in a situation where you can introduce people to each other, by all means do so. A person may attend an event and be too bashful to go right up and introduce herself to people she doesn't know. Go out of your way to introduce people to each other. Tell each person what the other does for a living and highlight a couple of his interests.

Once, after receiving a referral from someone I had met only once, I asked why he thought of me. He replied that he had attended a meeting of an association to which I belong. It was his first time there, and while everyone else practically ignored him, I made him feel like part of the crowd, introducing him around and making sure he was always involved in the conversation.

Little things like that get noticed and definitely help you in *Winning Without Intimidation.*

### The one "key" question

In *ENDLESS REFERRALS . . .* , I bring up what I call the "one key question" that will set you apart from all the rest. It will also help you Win Without Intimidation in the long-term—and sometimes right away, depending on the circumstances.

After finding out what a person does for a living and asking a couple of what I call "open-ended, feel-good questions," which spur them to say more about what they do, while feeling good about themselves in the process, I ask the following: "Joe, how can I know if someone I'm talking to would be a good prospect for you?"

Think about what your response would be if someone asked you, "How can I know if someone I'm talking to would be a good prospect for you?" What would you think?

142

How would you feel?

That's a question that will never offend anyone, but it will always be much appreciated. Most people have never been asked *that* question, and knowing you are a possible referral source—or even cared enough to ask—will certainly make them want to go out of their way to please you. If you can ever do it, make sure to actually refer business their way.

You can also adapt the essential premise of that question to any particular situation in which you are involved. For instance, "Hey, Mary, how can I know if someone I'm talking to would be a good contact for you in helping your son find a summer job?"

Even if you never successfully deliver a referral, Mary will hold you in high regard and most likely be happy to assist you in your endeavors.

### Addressing the superior

There are times you must go over a person's head (nicely, of course) and summon the manager.

You can do this tactfully by saying, "I understand you want to help and that it's a tough situation. I certainly don't want to get you in hot water. I'd actually feel more comfortable discussing this with your manager." Make sure to ask the manager's name—including her last name—before she is summoned.

When the manager arrives, she may assume you're like most people—ready to take her head off. Don't be surprised if she starts out a bit defensively. Your attitude with the person who had to get her will probably help, but assume he just went back and like most people said, "We have a customer with a problem."

Realize you may be dealing with a person who is expecting an argument. Have your sincere, warm smile ready to disarm. Say, "Hi, Ms. Jackson." (Please, use last names whenever you can. It shows respect.) Shake her hand with a firm, but non-aggressive grip. Smile and look

143

in her eyes as you say her name.

"I'm Bob Burg, Thank You for seeing me, I know you're very busy."

What have you done? Totally disarmed that person and put her in a win/win frame of mind. Now you can make your case on a level playing field. Or better, one slanted significantly in your favor.

### Giblin's truth serum

In Les Giblin's book *How To Have Confidence And Power In Dealing With People*, he shows that the best way to get someone to act in a particular way is to let them "live up" to your opinion of them. He provides several wonderful examples of people who were trusted and lived up to the trust placed in them.

One story tells of a police officer who was consistently able to get thugs to give him information by saying, "People tell me you have quite a reputation as a tough guy and that you've been in lots of trouble, but there's one thing you won't do. You won't lie. They say, if you tell me anything at all, it will be the truth—and that's the reason I'm here." Wow, talk about giving a person something to live up to!

Les quotes famed British statesman Sir Winston Churchill as saying, "I have found that the best way to get another to acquire a virtue, is to impute it to him."

As I've suggested, gear these techniques to your own unique circumstances. Not just to see if they work—they work!—but to practice getting really good at making them work for you in a variety of situations. I couldn't wait to try this technique. My first opportunity was with a person trying to get some information for me.

I had used her services before and she always did a good job. Not great, but good. She was having some trouble this particular time and I said to the person next to me, "I don't know if this information can be found or not, but I'll tell you this—if anyone can find it, she can."

144

You can bet your boots she found it, and now she goes out of her way for me whenever I need to stop by.

### The "Negative Yes"

I learned this next technique from the great speaker and sales trainer Tom Hopkins, author of the outstanding book, *How To Master The Art Of Selling*. Tom suggests, when trying to set an appointment for something that a person usually resists, phrasing your question in the form of a negative so that a "No" answer serves the same purpose as a "Yes" response. This works best when the person is used to saying, and almost automatically answers, "No."

Confusing? Here's how it works:

A realtor wanting to visit a seller who is planning to sell her home without professional assistance, might ask over the telephone, "Ms. Davis, would you be offended if I popped by to see your home?" When she says, "No," she's really saying "Yes, come on over."

Had he said the usual, "May I stop by to see your home?," then the "No" answer would have truly meant no. The "negative yes" technique won't work every time, but it will swing the odds more in your favor.

When attempting to Win Without Intimidation by getting a person to consider something you need, simply ask, "Would you be offended if . . . ?" and finish your request. There's a very good chance you'll get a "No" which, of course, means a winning "Yes!"

### Quick tip—Plant the affirmative

When asking a person a question for which you'd like a "Yes" response, learn to naturally nod your head up and down as you complete your question. If he's "on the fence" regarding an issue, that little nod might just pull him over to your side.

The technique of planting the affirmative also lends itself to the way you ask a question. Let me give you a sort of facetious example for this one:

Let's say you're going to ask someone out on a dinner date. Which of these three ways do you think would elicit the most positive response:

#1. "You wouldn't want to go out to dinner with me, would you?"

#2. "Would you like to go out to dinner with me?"

#3. "If we were to go to dinner, where would you most like to go?"

Number three is the only question that is set up so that within the answer is the "Yes" response. If the person you are asking responds by saying, "Oh, I'd like to go to the Lobster House Restaurant," they have actually said, "Yes, I'd like to go out with you . . . to the Lobster House Restaurant."

I've personally never asked a woman out that way. I'm not that brave! But you know, it might be fun to see what happens . . .

### Getting the cab driver on your side

If you are leaving your hotel in the morning and catching a cab to the airport, here's a way to get the driver on your side, have a smooth, pleasant ride and ensure that you're treated right. As you leave the hotel, offer the cab driver a cup of coffee.

Usually the hotels offer free coffee in the morning and it's okay to take one for the driver. Even if you do have to pay for it, it's still a good investment. You're most likely the only passenger who has ever shown the driver such respect and he'll really appreciate it. It isn't a bad idea to have him on your side to get around that rush hour traffic.

### Compliment the uncomplimented

Go out of your way to compliment those people who serve others but are not usually treated with respect. From the waitperson to the skycaps—aside from tipping—do you refer to them as sir or ma'am? Yes, it makes

146

a definite difference in how far out of their way they'll go for you.

A great illustration of *Winning Without Intimidation* by complimenting the uncomplimented showcases the abilities of the great former quarterback—and highly successful entrepreneur—Fran Tarkenton.

As a quarterback, and a small one at only 5'10", Fran was always the target of the huge, tough, often merciless defensive linemen. Linemen can be mean to a quarterback. They're supposed to be. It's their job. On top of that, they know they don't earn the kind of money most quarterbacks make and they certainly don't enjoy the same praises and glory. Those 300 pound guys can be downright rough to the Fran Tarkentons of the world.

But Fran is a master at dealing with people—and *Winning Without Intimidation*. After a play, he'd acknowledge his attacker by saying something like, "Great day for football, isn't it?" or "Man, that was quite a hit."

These guys weren't exactly used to quarterbacks actually talking to them—in more than four letter words—and they certainly weren't used to being treated as human beings. Before long, they weren't quite as aggressive, mean and nasty with Fran.

They'd still hit him, but they wouldn't rough him up as they did other quarterbacks. He took the anger out of them and probably added years to his Hall of Fame career.

Wow, that's when *Winning Without Intimidation* really comes in handy—when your life depends upon it!

### Shaking hands

The way you shake hands *is* important. Typically, a firm but not crunching or aggressive handshake is best; look the person in the eye and smile a genuine happy-to-meet-you smile.

Dad taught us how to shake hands and introduce ourselves when we were still practically babies, and that's a skill I've often been complimented on throughout my life.

147

Another great way of shaking hands I've learned from observing successful people is to use a double hand clasp, your hands sandwiching theirs, and give a slight bow of your head. That tells a person they must be very special.

It's another win, *hands down.*

### Quick tip—Attitude

When you're about to solicit someone's help, assume that person will be helpful instead of obstructive. Whichever attitude you expect *him* to take will show up in *your* attitude toward him, and he will usually respond according to your attitude.

It's just another case of getting what you expect.

### Re-introduce yourself

Making other people feel comfortable with you is one sure step to both short- and long-term *Winning Without Intimidation.* One great way to do this is to reintroduce yourself to people you've previously met—even if they *should* know your name.

We all forget names sometimes, and one of the most uncomfortable feelings in the world is to have someone approach you whose name you should know—and *you don't.* It's even worse if you're with one or two people to whom you're expected to introduce this person.

Has anyone ever approached you whose name you couldn't remember?

Have you ever approached someone who should know your name, but she doesn't? You are either sure she doesn't remember, or you're not sure, but you suspect it?

Here's the most effective way I know to handle this situation, and you'll score big points with that person: Simply reintroduce yourself. It's as easy as that.

"Hi, Joe, Bob Burg." Or even, "Hi, Nancy, Bob Burg, we met at the save-a-pet fundraiser two weeks ago."

What I've done is given that person an "out." I've allowed her—and her ego—to save face. Now she doesn't have to be uncomfortable with me or herself. And she'll usually respond by saying, "Sure, Bob, I remember you."

I know she didn't remember me. And she knows she didn't remember me. She might even know that *I know* she didn't remember me. It doesn't matter. Making that reintroduction will most definitely re-establish the person's "know you, like you, trust you" feelings, and will help you on your way to *Winning Without Intimidation.*

### F-O-R-M

A great idea, developed by super-entrepreneur Dexter Yager and brought to my attention several years ago, is the F-O-R-M method of asking questions. This acronym helps focus your attention on what might be important to the other person by knowing that:

"F" stands for (their) Family.

"O" stands for (their) Occupation.

"R" stands for (their) favorite types of Recreation.

"M" stands for (their) Message, what they deem important.

If you want to learn more, but they've stopped talking, just say, "Really, tell me more. . . ." When was the last time you had a conversation with someone who was so genuinely curious about you he or she wanted to know *more?*

When you focus on "FORM" during a conversation, you'll always be talking about the other person's favorite subject—and that always leads to *Winning Without Intimidation.*

### Quick tip—Understanding

You've seen throughout this book how people like to feel as though they are heard and understood. Regardless of the situation, people will make more of an effort on your behalf when they feel you understand their personal challenges regarding a situation. Make it a point not only to understand that person, but to understand in such a way that the person *knows* you understand. That can make all the difference in the world in your attempts at *Winning Without Intimidation.*

### Solicit their opinion

When trying to convince people of your point of view and persuading them to take the action you want, you'll find that the more you ask them for their opinion and counsel, the more they'll be on your side.

One of the best examples of this I ever saw was years ago at a college speech given by Senator Ted Kennedy.

Facing a crowd that was somewhat challenging in nature, the senator took an informal poll regarding an issue that was very controversial at that time. He actually asked the audience members who felt a certain way about the subject to raise their hands. He made the audience feel as though he was asking for, and actually *cared* about, our opinion. From that point on, the audience was much more receptive.

Have you ever heard the saying "People don't care how much you know, until they know how much you care?" The senator did just that with the entire audience.

I've used the technique of soliciting advice from prospects (whether or not I always felt I needed it) and others throughout the years, and it's most definitely served as a very effective tool for *Winning Without Intimidation.* After attaining the desired results, always make that person feel as though the ideas were theirs and that they contributed greatly to your success.

The more you ask, the more, in fact, you actually *will* learn and the chances are good they will end up making a contribution to your success.

Les Giblin suggests asking someone for "advice" instead of a "favor." That's an excellent idea. Think of an example: You want to get your son a summer job at the McJones company and a neighbor of yours—who you know by name, but don't know that well—is in upper management there and could probably help.

You correctly feel it would be too presumptuous of you to simply walk up and ask him to get your boy a job, so you ask him for advice. "Don, if you don't mind my asking, if you were me and were going to attempt to get your son set up with a summer job at the McJones Company, how do you feel would be the most effective way to go about it?"

Don, who is now being asked for counsel—not a favor—might just tell you to send your son to his office on Monday, and he'll see what he can do—or maybe he'll give you the personnel manager's name and number and tell you to use him as a referral. At worst, he'll lead you in the right direction.

Just remember to phrase your request something similar to: "Phyllis, if your were me and were attempting to _____ , how would you go about it?" or "Joe, I'd like to get your opinion on something. What would you do if blah, blah, blah?"

It's another way to set up a big win.

### Don't embarrass someone by "catching" them

Does it ever do any good to embarrass someone, either publicly or privately? I don't believe it does anytime, but especially if you are ever planning to win this person over without intimidation. Embarrassing a person by "catching" them at something is a sure way to shoot yourself in the foot—or worse.

I was in a conversation with a group of several people at a social gathering and when asked a question, I answered by repeating a very funny line I had heard on a recent TV show. Everyone laughed, and , I admit, I accepted the laughter without explaining that I borrowed that joke.

One of the people in the group had seen the same program and called me on it in front of everyone. It was embarrassing, and although I was wrong to not give credit to the show, it certainly did not endear that person to me.

What did that person gain by embarrassing me? Nothing but perhaps an instant—and very fleeting—moment of satisfaction. Remember the ego?

On the other hand, at college, we had a guest speaker named Bill Lee. Bill was a former major league pitcher known as "Spaceman" for his unusual personality. Before the speech, about 30 of us had a private welcoming party for Bill.

At that party, I said something meant to be funny that just didn't go over, and the room was silent. It was one of those longer-than-forever *embarrassing* silences. Bill stepped right in and segued from my dumb joke into a story, which totally took the heat off of me and took the embarrassing feeling right away. Understandably, from that point on I've been a big Bill Lee fan.

### What *not* to do in order to Win Without Intimidation

At some of my speaking engagements, my clients will assign a host to make sure I get to where I need to be and am taken care of during my stay. One client of mine in particular provides this courtesy quite often, for which I'm very grateful, and the hosts are always nice people who go out of their way to make sure all is okay, from accommodations to transportation.

After one of my late presentations, my host and I went to the hotel restaurant, which had just closed, to see if we could get a couple of sandwiches. Typically, I'm too keyed up before a program to eat, but afterwards I'm often very hungry. I sure could have used a sandwich right about then. By the time we got to the restaurant, the only person in the front dining room was the manager. Everyone else was either gone or in the kitchen cleaning up. The manager was across the room from us, and my host—a really nice guy—got the manager's attention by yelling, "Yo!"

Being a *Winning Without Intimidation* type guy, I was

152

immediately embarrassed. It was obvious the manager wasn't any more pleased than I. As he turned around, I could see a very annoyed look on his face which seemed to say, "I can't believe I have to put up with people like that." He didn't actually say that, but the expression on his face sure did.

He responded by sarcastically saying, "Yo! How can I help you?" Funny, when my host asked if we could get a couple of sandwiches, the answer was they were already closed. Surprise! Surprise!

I was able to eventually get the sandwiches made, but I really had to work for that one. First by undoing the damage done by my well-intentioned host, and then winning over—without intimidation, of course—the manager.

Finally, he told me that if the ingredients had not yet been put away, he would see to it that we got them. But how unnecessary that challenge was, when a simple, respectful greeting in the first place would have done the trick and made for an easy win.

### Even kids can Win Without Intimidation

My sister Robyn related this story to me about my eight year old niece, Samantha. I was very proud of the way she handled the following situation:

Samantha had one of her little girlfriends over to the house to play. They were getting along fine when the friend began to get cranky, as eight year olds will. They had agreed to go outside to play when all of a sudden the little friend yelled, "I'm not going outside to play with you!"

Sami kept her head—responding, not reacting—and nicely said, "Okay, well I'm going outside anyway," and began to walk away. She took a couple more steps and just before she reached the door she stopped, turned around and said, "but it won't be as much fun without you."

According to Robyn, the little friend's eyes just lit up, and she decided to join my niece outside. Robyn said she thought I'd be proud of Sami for that. Although I'm always proud of her—and my nephew, Mark—I was especially proud of the way she utilized the art of *Winning Without Intimidation.*

### The positive challenge

Give a person a challenge framed in a positive manner and they will often go out of their way for you in order to meet that challenge.

My good friend Monte Johnson, and his wife Cindy, needed quick invitations to a wedding shower. They were having no success at all with the local printers. Cindy was pleading, "We really need to get these today. We're in an emergency situation." The response: There was no way they could possibly do that.

If you look at this situation closely, you can see that when Cindy said, "We really need to get these today," she was actually being "I" oriented, which should be okay in this case, since she's the paying customer. But as we discover every day, people don't do things logically, but emotionally.

Monte—who intuitively employs a lot of the techniques we've been discussing in this book—told me he got on the phone with the next printer and simply asked, "What's the fastest you've ever gotten invitations out?" The response was, "Oh, we can probably get them out today."

Isn't that amazing?

It doesn't surprise those of us who use these methods every day. This is simply the way to win—without intimidation. What was the difference in focus in the way that Monte made his request?

He was "You" oriented. "What's the fastest *you've* ever gotten invitations out?"

Monte, who is in video production and tapes large conventions, often finds himself in a new town and may need to get an item in a hurry, such as a banner. He'll call a company that supplies banners and asks, "If there's any way you could help me out—this just got dropped on my lap and your help would really be appreciated. In fact, if there's any extra charge, that's fine."

Monte tells me—and I believe it because I do this myself all the time—his success rate is almost 100 percent and he hardly ever has to pay anything extra.

### Giving before getting

In *Winning Without Intimidation* over the long haul, you'll find that the more you're willing to give to others—without expecting anything—the more you'll get in return. A great example of this is my friend and client, Ron Hale of Tennessee. Ron is an extremely successful businessman who practiced the art of giving without expecting instant rewards while still in the armed forces.

As an Air Force recruiter, Ron's job was basically to sell young people on why they should join the service and serve their country while creating a good foundation in life for themselves. Before he could sell them on anything, however, he first had to get in front of them, and that could be a difficult task. To make matters even more challenging, he was located in a town that was filled with *Navy* people.

Ron knew that one key to his success was developing centers of influence who could serve as good sources of referrals—people who might actually send good candidates to him. But how could he develop relationships with these centers of influence without becoming a bother to them, causing negative feelings?

Here's where Ron perfectly used his natural inclination to give without expecting a return. Still, the result would be countless referrals and opportunities for free publicity from some of the most important centers of influence in town.

During his weekly itinerary, Ron would visit such places as schools, radio stations, television stations and the local newspaper. When stopping by, he would never mention anything about recruiting or referrals. He would simply strike up a friendly chat and then find a way he could help *them*.

For instance, he would bring the person at the radio station the newest air force band records for them to play whenever they liked. To the administrators and teachers at the schools, he'd bring in Air Force book covers that would help prolong the life of the books. There was a young minister with a very small television station which was often left with lots of dead air time. What would Ron bring him? Air Force films with entertaining footage that could fill up lots of time. Every so often, the young, up-and-coming minister would run Air Force ads right on the air.

All the while, Ron never once asked for a referral. But to whom do you think those folks sent all the young people they felt should check out the armed services? Ron was building a huge referral business simply by cultivating "giving" relationships with these center-of-influence people.

One holiday season, the editor of the local newspaper in this primarily Navy town decided to ask an armed forces representative for a story regarding military personnel at Christmas. Instead of asking someone from the Navy, he asked Ron. Soon after that, Ron and his family were the focus of a feature story in that very same newspaper. According to Ron, that one story was worth its weight in gold in free advertising.

Remember the young television minister who Ron helped out by constantly bringing in films about the Air Force to help fill the dead air time? As he grew bigger and better known, he remembered Ron and gave him more and more free publicity. You'd probably agree that he actually got fairly big. His name is Pat Robertson.

I've had the pleasure of getting to know Ron, and his lovely wife Toby. They both embody the spirit of giving, and by consistently giving without expecting immediate results, have built an enormous network marketing organization that literally spans the globe.

Give, give, and give some more, and ultimately you will find yourself *Winning Without Intimidation* more than you ever thought possible.

### Saying "No" to charity telephone solicitations without intimidation

It happens to us all. In the middle of dinner or while relaxing with our family, the telephone rings, and on the other end is a nice person reading from a script asking us to make a financial donation to the very worthwhile charitable cause he or she is representing. That, in and of itself, is fine—providing it's a legitimate charity. If you want to make a donation to that particular cause, fantastic. I know that many of us truly enjoy donating to causes we believe in.

However, let's face it, even Bill Gates probably couldn't afford to donate a significant amount of money to every charitable organization in the world. I don't know about you, but it seems as though I'm called by just about every charitable organization in the world.

How do you say "No," nicely, without intimidation or being rude or slamming down the phone, discouraging another human being from doing their job. Here's how I do it, and it's proven to be very effective:

I let them finish their short presentation, and then respond by saying, "I appreciate your call. I do, however, have several charities to which I donate, and although I'm contacted by many very worthwhile causes, such as yours, I have made the decision to stick with the ones I've chosen." Then add, "But I do appreciate your call and wish you the best of success in your work. Thank you very much for your time."

Nine times out of ten, they'll thank you for *your* time and hang up. If they try one more time, such as, "Well, sir, just a very small donation would really help . . ." I let them complete their sentence and then say, "I appreciate your offer, but again, that is the decision I've made. Best of success, though. Have a great night."

That will do it. There's no reason to say you can't afford it, or anything else. That's not really any of anyone else's beeswax. The answer I just gave is polite, and encouraging, and more than satisfactory, because when you both can't win, making sure no one loses is a great second best.

Many times I've had telephone solicitors actually thank me for my politeness and encouragement instead of the rudeness they're often shown by people. What a great feeling to know you're making a positive difference in someone's life.

### Setting an example people will follow

My good friend Vic Landtroop related a couple of stories to me about how doing what is right—instead of what is usual—can be a positive influence which others will duplicate. Both examples happened at a college football game between two great rivals, the University of Florida and the University of Tennessee.

Vic and his business associate Bubba Pratt (who I mentioned earlier in the book), two of Bubba's young children and another friend, drove up from Florida to Tennessee in Bubba's custom built luxury coach to see the game. It would be a record-breaking crowd and the parking lot was filled to capacity with fans from both schools having a huge tail-gate party before the early afternoon game.

As Vic says, often in that kind of situation there's a lot of disrespect back and forth between the fans of the rival teams. In fact, three Tennessee Volunteer supporters who were drinking beer over their hibachi and already "feeling their oats," looked over and made a somewhat sarcastic remark about the Florida Gators. Vic and Bubba decided to take the high road and Win Without Intimidation.

Bubba and Vic were complimentary toward the other team. "We have a lot of respect for the guys on your team," they told the Tennessee fans. "They're super folks in our eyes." They approached the situation the right way—not out of weakness, but out of strength. (Incidentally, Bubba is a former Gator linebacker and a martial artist, and Vic is a former professional wrestler!)

Remember the saying by Simeon ben Zoma, "A mighty person is one who can control their emotions and make of an enemy a friend." That's just what Vic and Bubba did. In fact, they invited the three guys to tour Bubba's custom coach and even offered them some of the food they'd laid out. They treated their guests with class.

Vic says, "It was great—despite the 'cans of courage' those fellows had been drinking, they kept telling us what super guys we were."

After the game, which Florida won, the three Volunteer fans sought Vic and Bubba out and complimented them on the Gator win with comments such as, "Hey, the best team won. We hope you go all the way."

What a great job by Vic and Bubba of setting a positive example—an example others can follow—by treating people with respect, instead of falling into the reactive trap of "insult and rivalry." I believe Vic and Bubba's attitude really set the stage for influencing the behavior of those other fans.

Vic related another story to me, which shows the same kind of positive impact you can have when you choose to lead in a positive direction.

As the fans were walking to the stadium, they had to come down a very steep slope in the pathway. Bubba—who's a real gentleman—first noticed that the men were not helping the women, some of whom were having trouble with their footing on the steep grade. According to Vic, "It was just like every man—and woman—for themselves.

As soon as Bubba started helping people, practically everyone else, men and women alike, began lending a helping hand."

Isn't it great to know we can all make a real difference by reaching out just a little? People will follow others who set a positive example.

Vic says we all need to read *How To Win Friends and Influence People,* and other books on personal growth. "I never knew about these tools when I was growing up," he told me. "I'm glad to be raising my kids where I'm able to expose them to these resources while they're still young."

*Winning Without Intimidation* for generations to come. What a great concept!

**The importance of humor in *Winning Without Intimidation***

Maybe it goes without saying but very often, humor—kind humor, not sarcastic humor—can go a long way toward *Winning Without Intimidation* and getting what you want.

I'm very comfortable with self-deprecating humor. In a tense situation, I make myself the object of the humor. "Umh, I can't believe I lost this ticket. I literally would lose my head if it weren't attached to my neck." That puts the other person just a little bit closer to my side of the challenge.

If you're not comfortable laughing at yourself (I am because there's a lot to laugh about), make fun of the situation itself—*only,* of course, if that's appropriate and will help your cause. If you're not a naturally funny or humorous person, please don't force humor—it will have the opposite effect. However, if you can downplay the seriousness or make light of the situation, it will definitely help you in your quest toward *Winning Without Intimidation.*

**Treat your suppliers the same way you treat your customers and clients**

To ensure a wonderful relationship with your suppliers, one in which you get special, preferential treatment—especially in those situations where it is badly needed—be sure to build a strong foundation. You can do that easily by treating them with all the respect most people normally reserve only for their paying customers.

Do you pay your suppliers on time?

Do you talk *to* them instead of *at* them?

Do you discuss challenges, instead of demanding and yelling?

Do you refer others to them, if and when appropriate?

If you answered "Yes" to those questions, you are on your way to earning that special place in their hearts which will elicit consistent efforts on your behalf—especially in those minor emergencies where the average person may not get that same satisfaction.

That's the essence of *Winning Without Intimidation*.

**Keeping cool behind the wheel**

Although you might not immediately recognize the name of my good friend Ralph Lagergren, you may have read about him in PEOPLE magazine, or read the book based on the success story of Ralph and his cousin, Mark Underwood.

Mark invented—and Ralph sold and marketed—a more efficient grain reaper that could outperform the standard machines sold by the larger, more established farm implement companies. The book about their venture, *Dream Reaper,* written by Craig Canine, is great reading. It's truly an American success story involving our wonderful system of free enterprise and the good that can result when you combine a big dream with ingenuity and hard work.

Ralph is one of those guys you immediately like, and a man who also believes in the benefits of *Winning Without*

161

*Intimidation.* One day, Ralph was driving along with his two kids and stopped at a red light. Behind him was a man driving a Volkswagen, and through his rear view mirror Ralph could tell the guy was mad at him. Although Ralph didn't know what he had done to elicit such angry feelings—possibly he stopped too short or too abruptly—he could see the man gesturing and mouthing words that didn't look like roses, if you know what I mean.

Ralph is a big ol' Kansas cowboy and not the type you want to pick a fight with. But he also had two young children in the car with him, and anyway, Ralph would rather do his *Winning Without Intimidation.*

When the light turned green, Ralph began driving and could see right away the Volkswagen pulling up to him. Ralph warned the kids that this man might make an unfriendly gesture and that the three of them would respond with a friendly smile and a wave. That's exactly what happened and, according to Ralph, the face of the man in the Volkswagen turned from angry to somewhat confused.

Wouldn't you know that at the next traffic signal the light turned red, and the two cars pulled up right next to each other. When the man looked over, a bit embarrassed, Ralph smiled that big ol' cowboy smile at him again. The man, startled again, asked if they knew each other. Ralph replied, "No, we don't know each other, but life is just too short to let things like traffic misunderstandings get in the way of enjoying myself."

Two months later, Ralph was stopped at another red light, driving a different car. All of a sudden, that same Volkswagen pulled up beside him and the man in the car, remembering his face, waved and smiled at his new friend.

What an excellent example Ralph set for his children on how, with a little bit of thought and effort, one person can make the world a better place for others as well as oneself. Ralph was the mightier man, wasn't he? Because he controlled his emotions and made of an enemy a friend. That's *Winning Without Intimidation!*

### *Winning Without Intimidation* to get backstage
Here's another Ralph Lagergren story:

Ralph's wife Dawn is a big fan of country singer and musician George Strait. When the former Entertainer of the Year was making an appearance in Ralph's town, Ralph thought of a great surprise he could give his wife . . . an opportunity to meet Mr. Strait backstage before his concert. Aside from the fact that lots of people would like to get backstage at concerts, Ralph knew that another major challenge is that this singing superstar has a policy of seeing only two guests backstage per performance.

Ralph, a master at *Winning Without Intimidation*, sent a letter to the sponsoring radio station expressing that through thick and thin, good times—and especially the tough times—Dawn had stood by him. It would be a very special gift to her if she could get a chance to meet Mr. Strait. He added, "I'm not worried about meeting him myself, as I know he only sees two people per show, but it would be just great if I could get this for Dawn."

The station manager called Ralph, saying he had received the letter and found it very interesting and certainly moving. Ralph replied—and these words are key— *"I want to thank you for even considering this.* I know it's difficult for you and there must be thousands of requests like mine. This would just be so special for her."

You can guess the results, can't you? Those words, *"I want to thank you for even considering this,"* work like magic. You are being humble and respectful.

Will it always work? No, not always. Sometimes the situation just won't allow it. However, if there's any chance at all, those words will usually cinch it for you.

At the concert, the public address announcer paged Ms. Dawn Lagergren, asking her to come backstage. What an incredible surprise and gift Ralph was able to give to his best friend and loving wife, because he had mastered the art of *Winning Without Intimidation.*

### The *Winning Without Intimidation* dream

I'm the type that really gets into my work. When I was writing this book, the topic of *Winning Without Intimidation* consumed my mind—literally day and night—to the point that I was waking up during the night writing down ideas that would come to me while I was sleeping, and even having story-like dreams about this book. One of these dreams really made me laugh. It was strange, but really brought up a worthwhile point I want to share with you.

In this dream, there was a helmet with strange powers. Anyone who wore this helmet automatically knew the perfect *Winning Without Intimidation* response to a challenging situation, and was in the proper mindset to enact it. When you took the helmet off, that was no longer so, but when you put it back on, you again had the benefits of that super power.

I laughed during my dream, because when someone had a challenge with someone else, she would ask for the helmet, put it on, and handle every situation beautifully.

Weird dream? Sure. Weird guy—weird dream. But I believe the point is this: If we, whenever a challenge with someone comes up, decide to respond by putting on that helmet before reacting negatively, we will always be in a position of strength—knowing exactly what to say and how to say it—consistently *Winning Without Intimidation.*

### The language of strength

I want to end by reiterating a way to handle yourself and deal with those difficult others I mentioned near the beginning of this book. It may be the one concept that makes the biggest difference in your ability to persuade others to your way of thinking, and attain the results you desire. It is known by several different words: diplomacy, delicacy, sensitivity, savior faire, and *tact*.

Tact is the inspired language of strength. Learning what to say and how to say it will get results for you which will seem just like magic.

Every situation you find yourself in, and every time you must call someone's attention to a particular way of acting, keep tact in mind. Tact will be the key to how those people receive you and what you say, and whether that person will ultimately take the action that will benefit all concerned.

When you master the art of tact, you will constantly and consistently find yourself in the position of *Winning Without Intimidation*.

Just think for a moment: How many of us will it take—no longer reacting, but responding to the challenges in our work and lives and *Winning Without Intimidation*—to change the world for the better forever ... ?